The Quest for Peace between Israel and the Palestinians

Haig Khatchadourian

The Quest for Peace between Israel and the Palestinians

WIPF & STOCK · Eugene, Oregon

Wipf and Stock Publishers
199 W 8th Ave, Suite 3
Eugene, OR 97401

The Quest for Peace between Israel and the Palestinians
By Khatchadourian, Haig A.
Copyright©2000 by Khatchadourian, Haig A.
ISBN 13: 978-1-61097-057-0
Publication date 5/1/2011
Previously published by Peter Lang, 2000

To the memory of my parents and
uncles and aunts who are no more

Contents

Acknowledgments	ix
Introduction	xi
1. The Palestine Problem and the Arab-Israeli Conflict: A Historical Sketch	1
2. Territorial Rights of Palestinians and Jews	21
3. Proposals for Peace between Palestinians and Israel, and the Future of Jerusalem	39
4. From Autonomy to Independence	69
5. Israel and the Arab Countries in the Quest for Peace	95
6. The Peace Dividend	115
7. Liberalization, Democratization, and Stability in the Arab Middle East	129
8. Conclusion	155
Index	165

Acknowledgments

The author wishes to thank Lynne Rienner Publishers, Inc., for permission to include quotations from Yvonne Yazbeck Haddad's article, "Islamists and the Peace Process," in *Political Islam, Revolution, Radicalism, or Reform?* (1997), edited by John L. Esposito.

Introduction

The quest for a just, comprehensive, and lasting peace in the Middle East has been a very long, difficult, and painful quest, and although considerable progress toward such a peace has been made during the past few decades, and its realization now appears to lie in sight, it still eludes the efforts of politicians and everyday people in the region and in the world at large to bring it about. The present work presents and defends its author's vision of the shape of such a peace, and the road that he believes can lead the region toward that goal. At the center of that vision lie the lineaments of a free, independent Palestine on the West Bank and Gaza Strip, with East Jerusalem as its capital, coexisting in peace alongside Israel; although the very idea of a Palestinian state, or even a comprehensive peace between the Palestinians and Israel, is anathema to the radical Israeli right. Similarly, the idea of an Islamic state is abhorrent to the Palestinian and other Arab Islamists.

However, as this Introduction was being written, several noteworthy events took place which encourage one to believe that peace, at least between the Palestinians and Israel, may not be as far off as, in our more pessimistic moments, we may be inclined to think. One was Yasser Arafat's reaffirmation, during his latest visit to Washington on February 4, 1999, that despite the slump in the peace process, the "process of reconciliation with Israel [is] irreversible and the opening of a 'new chapter' in the troubled Middle East,"[1] and his "confidence in the Palestinians' achieving statehood . . . and that a Palestinian state would live side by side in peace and reconciliation with Israel."[2] Another encouraging note was President Clinton's reminding Arafat that although his administration "does not object to . . . assertions of Palestinian aspirations," "unilateral declarations of statehood 'aren't helpful.' "[3] Fortunately, the February 8 issue of *Time* reports that Arafat "has agreed to postpone the declaration of

Palestinian statehood he has repeatedly threatened to make on May 4, the date the interim Oslo peace accords expire. The timing became problematic once the Israelis scheduled elections for May 17."[4] Perhaps most surprising was the news that ultra-Orthodox rabbis, in talks with hard-line settler leaders, proposed that the latter "agree to a Palestinian state in exchange for more settlements"; that they "accept a radical increase in settlement in the West Bank—from about 150,000 to 600,000—as a trade-off for recognizing a Palestinian state with east Jerusalem as its capital. . . . But [Yaacov] Shulvitz [a follower of ultra-Orthodox leader Rabbi Eliezer Shach] said the proposal was 'just ideas' at the talking stage."[5] Although these are "just ideas," they are nonetheless significant in showing how the wind is beginning to blow: that at least some members of the Israeli ultra-right have begun to think the utterly unthinkable of a little while ago.

To help the reader place the subject of this work in its proper historical context, the book opens, in chapter 1, with a historical sketch of the Palestine Problem, the root cause of what eventually expanded into the general Arab-Israeli conflict. Next, in chapter 2, the territorial rights of Palestinians and Jews in the land of Palestine are assessed. It is argued that both Palestinians and Israelis have valid, perhaps roughly equal, moral and territorial rights based on their centuries-long occupation of the land in different periods of its checkered history; and consequently that the Palestinian/Jewish-Israeli conflict over territory is a conflict of right against right. Chapter 3 discusses and evaluates various proposals advanced by politicians, intellectuals, and scholars for the peaceful settlement of the Palestine Problem and defends the two state proposal favored by Yasser Arafat with the PLO's abandonment of its original aim of destroying Israel, and its de facto recognition of Israel's existence; although it also argues that Arafat's earlier (1970s) proposal—which called for a single, secular, democratic Palestinian-Jewish state in lieu of the Jewish state—although utterly impracticable, is fairer to the Palestinians than the two-state proposal.

Chapter 4 continues the defense of the two-state proposal begun in chapter 3 by responding to (a) a series of important Islamist criticisms of the Oslo Accords and the Palestinian autonomy that followed them, and (b) the hard-line position of the Israeli rejectionists. It argues that, contrary to what the latter believe, a Palestinian state would be the natural next step to the present limited Palestinian autonomy. It then critically evaluates some suggested ways of marginalizing the Islamists and the Israeli rejectionists.

Introduction

Chapter 5 briefly traces Israel's relations with Egypt, Syria, Lebanon, and Jordan, and Saudi Arabia's indirect relations with Israel through its relations with those Arab states that have been actors in the Arab-Israeli conflict. The aim of that survey is to ascertain the actual and possible ways in which some or all of these inter-state relations contribute to the quest for a comprehensive Middle East peace.

Chapter 6 deals with three related subjects: (a) the economic benefit or "peace dividend" that has accrued to Israel and, to a much lesser extent, to Egypt, Jordan, the Palestinians, and some other Arab countries, in the wake of the peace process; (b) the claim that the economic benefit resulting from bilateral and regional agreements and cooperation between Israel and the Arab countries would tend to decrease the regime of violence between them; and (c) the further "peace dividend"—the economic and cultural benefits—that the present author believes can and ought to accrue to Arabs and Israelis with the achievement of an overall settlement of the Arab-Israeli conflict.

I mentioned that one of the main claims evaluated in chapter 6 is the possible conflict-reducing role of bilateral and regional economic agreements and cooperation between the Arab countries and Israel, in light of the economic benefits to the parties. Chapter 7 pursues the theme of conflict-reduction by attempting to answer a different question; viz., whether, as has been claimed, political liberalization and democratization in the Arab countries may reduce the regime of war between them and Israel, and help bring about diplomatic efforts to address the conflict's underlying causes. A critical examination of that claim shows that (a) the connection between democracy and the absence of war in general is based on solid historical evidence, but that (b) the claim that under specified conditions that relation is likely to hold in the case of the Arab countries that are still at war with Israel, is more speculative. However, an important corollary of (b), namely that, other things being equal, democratization would tend to make the Middle East politically more stable or less unstable, is independently supported by the evidence that democracy legitimates political power and authority. That evidence, together with the fact that democracy is the political system most conducive to the individual's fullest development and actualization, and to the attainment of the general welfare, strongly argues for its desirability in the Arab world as a whole.

The preceding leads to the question of how democracy can best be established in the Middle East Arab countries, given the absence of a liberal political tradition, and some modest and tentative ideas as to how it may naturally grow, or be helped to grow, from the traditional culture, are presented. Also explored in relation to that question: the possible role of the traditional ethic/morality of honor, dishonor, and shame, and whether any forms of Islamic state may be compatible with democracy.

The desirability of democracy for the Arab/Muslim world is strongly challenged by the Islamists, who either reject "Western-style" democracy out of hand as alien to and unsuited for the Arabs, or else contend that Islam itself is authentically democratic. In either case their goal is to establish true Islamic regimes all over the Arab/Muslim world, squarely based on the principles of Islamic Law. In response to that challenge, appeal is made to the inherent democratic values, which are independent of time and place, or culture.

A general Conclusion rounds off the work.

Notes

1 "Arafat says peace efforts must go on," *Milwaukee Journal-Sentinel*, February 5, 1999.

2 Ibid.

3 Ibid.

4 "Delayed Gratification For Yasser Arafat," February 8, 1999, issue, 14

5 "Rabbis' proposal backs Palestinian state," *Milwaukee Journal-Sentinel*, January 22, 1999.

Chapter 1

The Palestine Problem and the Arab-Israeli Conflict: A Historical Sketch

I

This chapter has two main aims: first, to provide a concise historical sketch of the Palestine Problem, including Palestinian and other Arab perceptions or beliefs regarding what Palestinians consider to be the grievous injustices that they have suffered in this century; from the Balfour Declaration and its antecedents to the present—including, among its highlights, the United Nations' Partition Plan, the creation of the state of Israel, and the latter's occupation of East Jerusalem, the West Bank, and Gaza Strip—until the recent partial Palestinian autonomy in the latter territories. Second, to attempt to assess the extent to which these perceptions or beliefs are morally and legally, as well as historically, justified.

II

The origins of the Palestinian people[1] are still a matter of historical uncertainty; though there are various hypotheses concerning it.[2] But it is a historical fact that the Palestinians, the great majority of whom have been Arabs, go back at least to the country's Arab conquest in 634 A.D.

Thus they have been the indigenous inhabitants and the great majority of the country's population for more than thirteen centuries. However, the expulsion of the Jews from Palestine in 70 A.D. was incomplete. A small number of Jews, and their descendants, continued to live in the land long before the influx of European Jews from the Diaspora during and after World War II. Yet even with that influx during the British Mandate, the Jewish community continued to constitute a small albeit growing minority of the country's population (see note 20). The significance of these facts for the territorial claims of Arabs and Jews will be considered in chapter 2.

On November 2, 1917, the Balfour Declaration burst like a bomb upon the scene. In a letter to Lord Rothschild, A.J. Balfour, then British Foreign Secretary, stated that he had been authorized by the British government to release a statement indicating that

> His Majesty's Government view with favor the establishment in Palestine of a national home for the Jewish people, and will use their best endeavours to facilitate the achievement of this object, it being clearly understood that nothing shall be done which may prejudice the civil and religious rights of existing non-Jewish communities in Palestine, or the rights and political status enjoyed by Jews in any other country.[3]

Discussions at cabinet level and consultation with Jewish leaders, including Dr. Chaim Weizmann, whom Groisser describes as "a leading British scientist and Zionist,"[4] helped negotiate the declaration.

The immediate question at this point concerns the legal and moral authority of Britain—which in November 1917 had not yet received a League of Nations mandate over Palestine—to promise the Jews a "national home" in a land that was not part of its own territory, and in complete disregard for the wishes of the country's Arab majority. But if the British government lacked the legal and moral authority in 1917 to promise the Jews a national home in Palestine, which should be evident, did it acquire such an authority after the end of World War I, when the League of Nations granted Britain a "Mandate over Palestine"? The answer, once again, is a clear "No," and for exactly the same reasons; just as no individual or group has the moral or legal right to give away, in any shape or form, something that is not hers or its own.[5]

Edward W. Said succinctly summarizes these points as follows:

> The Declaration was made (a) by a European power, (b) about a non-European territory, (c) in a flat disregard of both the presence and the wishes of the native majority resident in that territory, and (d) it took the form of a promise about the same territory to another foreign group, [6] so that this foreign group might, quite literally, *make* the territory a national home for the Jewish people.[7]

And

> Balfour's statements in the declaration take for granted the higher right of a colonial power to dispose of a territory as it saw fit. As Balfour himself averred,

this was especially true when dealing with such a significant territory as Palestine and with such a momentous idea as the Zionist idea, which saw itself as doing no less than reclaiming a territory promised originally by God to the Jewish people, at the same time as it foresaw an end to the Jewish problem.[8]

Thus the Balfour Declaration, and its aftermath, dramatize the arbitrariness with which the British government treated Palestine and the Palestinian majority.

I should add that my criticism of the British policy exemplified by the Balfour Declaration and the steps the British government took to implement it entails nothing concerning the moral rights of the Jewish people to a national homeland. As I shall argue in the next chapter, the Jews, like the Palestinians, have a significant moral stake in the land. Thus the criticisms are not directed at the creation of the state of Israel, and, *a fortiori*, at the original idea of a "national home" for the Jews in Palestine itself. Stated differently, my criticism is that "the end does not justify the means." As will be seen in the sequel, my views about the immediately preceding points diverge, over all, from those of Palestinians and other Arabs during the greater part of the century.[9]

What must have magnified the Arabs' deep sense of injustice, their consternation and suspicions about the Balfour Declaration, was that the latter came about almost simultaneously with the Bolsheviks' leakage of the secret Sykes-Picot agreement between Britain and France. Indeed, as Anthony Nutting states, the Arabs saw the situation as nothing short of betrayal; since during World War I they thought that the British had promised *them* certain parts of the Near East, *including Palestine*, in return for their help to defeat the Ottomans.[10]

The twists and turns of British foreign policy in its attempts to win Hussein ibn Ali, the Sherif of Mecca, to the British side in the war with Turkey, both before and after October 31, 1914, the day Turkey declared war against Britain and entered the war on Germany's side, are well-summarized by Anthony Nutting.[11] Nutting writes that in October 1914,

> On the outbreak of war between Britain and Germany, [Lord] Kitchener, now Secretary of State for War in the British Cabinet, sent Abdullah [one of Hussein's sons] a message to inquire whether, if Turkey joined Germany against Britain, the Grand Sherif would cast his lot with the Turks or with the British. . . . Britain was at war with a deadly enemy and needs the Arabs as her allies. This was the chance for which Hussein was waiting.[12]

As a result of further correspondence between Hussein and Britain in October 1915, Sir Henry McMahon, speaking for the British government, wrote to Hussein that "Britain would recognize the areas in the Sherif's previous note [i.e., "the proclamation of an Arab caliphate for Islam"] with the exception of certain areas . . . listed as (1) the Cilician districts of Mersin and Alexandretta, (2) Lebanon and parts of Syria west of a line between Aleppo and Damascus, and (3) Southern Iraq from Baghdad to Basra."[13]

More importantly, in February, 1915 Faisal, Hussein's son, brought back with him from Constantinople, where he had gone, a memorandum by the Arab leaders in Syria and Iraq "which made it clear that . . . [the Arab secret societies] were not going to commit themselves to an open revolt against the Turks without explicit British guarantees of their independence. The memorandum . . . demanded that Britain recognize the independence of Syria, Lebanon, *Palestine,* Iraq and the Arabian peninsula."[14]

Despite his repeated attempts, and Faisal's successful revolt against Turkey, Hussein failed to pin down Britain to a precise definition of frontiers. Nutting summarizes the final position as follows:

> The upshot of all this was very far from the precise definitions of the Damascus memorandum. Though nothing can excuse Britain's and France's subsequent deception of the Arabs by the secret Sykes-Picot agreement and the Balfour Declaration, it seems extraordinary that the Sheriff should have regarded these exchanges as an adequate guarantee on which to launch the Arab Revolt . . . . Hussein clearly wanted to believe in Britain's sense of fair play because he wanted the revolt, which depended entirely on supplies of British arms and ammunitions for its success.[15]

Another author, Alvin Z. Rubinstein, writing in *The Arab-Israeli Conflict,*[16] summarizes the situation thus:

> When war erupted in 1914, Britain and Ottoman Turkey found themselves on opposite sides. The British attempted to use any means, fair or foul, to turn the non-Turkish inhabitants of the empire, many of whom had been at the edge of rebellion even before the war began, against their increasingly harsh and capricious masters in Istanbul. In the course of this effort, the British made many promises, some of them mutually exclusive, to the Arabs and to the Jews. In return for aiding the British war effort against the Turks, London promised the Arabs political independence. The promise to the Jews, brokered by Dr. Weizmann, who as a chemist had aided the British war effort, was the Balfour Declaration of November 1917.[17]

More important for an understanding of the root causes of the Palestinian issue than the ambiguous and vague British promises to the Arabs,[18] were Arab perceptions of, or beliefs about, Britain's promises to them, and so, their anger when they discovered Britain's double dealing in relation to them and the Jews.

To my earlier charge that the British government lacked the legal or moral authority or right to promise the Jews a "national home" in Palestine, one might add the charge of Britain's failure to grant eventual independence to Palestine that the League of Nations, in mandating Britain and France to govern the Near East provinces of the former Ottoman Empire, wanted them to grant eventual independence to their inhabitants. In failing to grant independence to Palestine, Britain went against the very mandate in which the League of Nations granted it.[19] But as we shall see later, Britain did make a number of attempts to resolve the competing Arab and Jewish claims in the 1930s and 1940s by proposing various solutions which, had they been accepted by the opposing parties— in particular, by the Palestinian leaders—would have led to the country's independence. When Britain finally turned the Palestine Problem to the United Nations, the territorial dispute had become a violent conflict between the Palestinians and the Jews on the one hand, and between the two and Britain. (As an Englishman recently told the present author: "Do not blame us. We did our best.")

What Anthony Nutting calls "A footnote to the [20th century] history of Palestine," is *apropos* at this point, regarding "the road not taken" by history. Nutting writes:

> One curious reflection prompts itself. Had France and not Britain succeeded in grabbing Palestine after World War I, Palestine might well have become an independent Arab state in the same way as Syria and Lebanon . . . . Rather than a "national home" for the Jews, Palestine would have become a French protectorate. And, when the time came for the Arabs to rise and throw off the French yoke, the Palestine Arabs would have made common cause with their Lebanese and Syrian brothers in gaining their independence. With the state of Palestine preserved intact, the whole Middle East would then have gained in stability and in strength.[20]

It might be said in defense of the Balfour Declaration that Britain's pledge to the Jews, notwithstanding the vagueness of the words "a national home for the Jews," promised far less than what the Zionists were eager to understand by them; viz. Britain's commitment to the creation of an independent Jewish state, in part if not in the whole, of Palestine. Consequently, that any Jewish misapprehensions concerning British intentions could not be laid at Britain's door. Be that as it may, it is impossible to get round the fact that the vagueness of "national home" (which paralleled the vagueness of the earlier British promise, or "promise," to the Arabs) augured nothing but future trouble, and greatly contributed to what the Zionists perceived the promise to entail, or wanted to mean.

The Arabs lost no time dramatizing their strong opposition to the Balfour Declaration, Jewish immigration into the country, and the building of increasing numbers of so-called Jewish colonies, in the decades preceding Israel's independence.[21] Despite Arab protests, demonstrations, and other forms of resistance to British policy, including the massacre of Jews in Hebron, and guerrilla fighting against British forces in the 1930s, Arab farmers continued to sell their land to the Jews, lured by the high prices offered, until their leaders belatedly forbade it.

For their own political ends, Palestinian leaders and the leaders of the neighboring Arab states played a not insignificant role in what became, in the words of a distinguished Lebanese historian, a veritable catastrophe. They did so, first and foremost, by their outright rejection of the 1947 UN Partition Plan.[22] Had they accepted it, the Palestinians and Jews would have been spared the more than fifty years of conflict, enmity, hatred, and suffering that continue to this day.

I speak advisedly of the responsibility of the Palestinian leaders and the neighboring Arab states since it was they who decided the fate of the ordinary Palestinians throughout the mandatory period. For example, the latter were not given the opportunity, by means of referendums or plebiscites, to decide for themselves these and other crucial matters affecting their very existence. Worst of all, their leaders and the heads of the neighboring Arab states (with the exception of King Abdallah[23]) used the same arbitrary and highhanded way to decide for the Palestinian people in 1948, by invading the nascent state of Israel rather than accepting Partition. Had the Palestinian masses been given the opportunity of deciding whether or not to accept the plan, and a proper understanding of the nature and implications of accepting or rejecting it, in terms of their own best interests, it is just possible that the majority would have opted for an independent Palestinian state alongside a Jewish state, as envisaged by the Partition Plan.

It is clearly impossible, especially at this late date, to test the preceding contrary-to-fact supposition, which must forever remain a nagging and tantalizing "what if" for Palestinians and their descendants everywhere, and for the world.

The personal and political rivalries between the Palestinian leadership that, from 1920 on, helped prevent the creation of a Palestinian state in 1948 alongside the Jewish state, were, specifically, between two prominent and powerful Jerusalem Muslim families, the al-Husaini and the

Nashashibi families. In 1937 it led to the final Palestinian rejection of the Peel Commission report. The report proposed that "the Galilee, with the exception of Nazareth, and the north coastal plain [,] would be a Jewish state. The Arab state would include everything else, save for a wide corridor from Jerusalem to Jaffa, which, with the Nazareth enclave and bases on the sea of Galilee and at Aqaba, would remain in British hands. The Arab state was to be joined, though it was not specified exactly how, with Abdallah's realm in Transjordan."[24]

The proposal was rejected outright by Al-Husaini and the Arabs of Syria and Iraq, "because it granted . . . Jewish sovereignty in any part of Palestine. Publicly, Abdallah and the Nashashibis opposed it as well, but privately it was known that they favored the plan so long as Raghib an-Nashashibi would rule under Abdallah at the expense of the al-Husainis."[25]

The Zionists were also divided over the Peel commission report. The Arabs' general lack of realism and foresight continued to be clearly manifest in the post-Peel commission period. For instance, when, after 1937, the British agreed in principle to the main Arab demand of an independent state under majority rule, the Arabs refused to acknowledge any Jewish rights "to special protection and rights for the Jewish minority. In the end there was no agreement and the British dictated their own terms."[26] One casualty was the dropping of the idea of an independent Arab state, "at least for the time being. A White Paper containing these strictures [including British accession to Arab demands to end Jewish immigration and to curtail land sale to Jews] was issued in May 1939. . . . Both the Jews and the Arab Higher Committee rejected the White Paper."[27]

To top it all, Palestinian nationalists, led by Haj Amin al-Hussaini, sided with Nazi Germany and the Axis powers during the Second World War. In addition to its immorality, that action meant the loss of a valuable opportunity for the Arabs to fight on the Allies' side—which had just cause and at least one main right intention on their side, however morally flawed actual Allied fighting against the Axis powers came to be in terms of *jus in bello* rules. By contrast, the Jews seized the opportunity. A Jewish brigade was formed and fought alongside the Allies, gaining valuable experience with war that later served it well.

The same pattern of rejections, sometimes unilateral, sometimes bilateral, and deadlock over the country's future, was repeated in relation to Britain's final, failed attempt to solve the Palestine Problem: the Morrison-Grady Plan,[28] and "subsequent patchwork attempts to adjust it in various ways."[29] Finally, in May 1947, Britain turned the whole matter to the United Nations. On August 31, 1947, the United States Special Committee

Special Committee on Palestine recommended the principle of Partition. The Zionists but not the Arabs accepted it "with passion."[30]

What I said earlier should leave no doubt about the present author's position toward the Arabs' rejection of the Partition Plan (a position steadfastly held since the Plan was proposed, not in hindsight), and their grave mistake in not accepting the creation of a Palestinian state alongside Israel in 1948. In fact, it has been claimed that by rejecting the Plan, the Palestinians not only missed a one-time chance but, in effect, forfeited their right to any part of the territory, thereby giving Israel the moral if not the legal right to the country as a whole. That view is without merit, as I shall argue in chapter 3.

Nevertheless, the unrelenting bombast and rhetoric of Arab leaders in 1948, 1967, and 1973 about their vaunted military prowess and alleged ability to defeat the Jewish state with ease, repeatedly fed false hopes to the Palestinian masses, and were constantly dashed to the ground. It also helped to make the Arabs their own greatest enemy. In 1991, siding with Saddam Hussein against Kuwait during the Gulf War[31]—although a psychologically understandable expression of frustration and anger at their miserable condition—the Palestinians in the occupied territories again showed that they could be swayed by external Arab blandishments, despite their belated awakening to the fact they themselves had to forge their own destiny; that they must rely on themselves first and foremost—perhaps themselves alone. I refer, among other things, to the grass roots movement known as the "intifada."[32] That lesson was forgotten by Yasser Arafat and the general Palestinian populace when they supported Saddam Hussein during the Gulf War, which gained nothing but misery for the Palestinians residing in Kuwait. Still, the Palestinians demonstrated a new determination to fashion their own destiny, reflected in the peace conferences in which they later effectively and successfully participated. They also proved in other ways that grass roots Palestinians, when pushed long and hard against the wall, can act: in this case, both through civil disobedience, stone throwing, and other low-level forms of freedom fighting.

We must not, of course, forget Palestinian terrorism as an even earlier form of grassroots resistance to the occupation than the freedom fighting of the intifada.[33] But I believe it was the Israeli invasion of Lebanon in 1982, together with Israel's attempts to crush the *Intifada*—certainly not terrorism—that turned the tide of world opinion toward greater understanding of and sympathy, or empathy, with the Palestinians' plight and the justice of their cause.

The Palestinian people have paid a very heavy price for their erstwhile naivete, political inexperience, lack of foresight, and gullibility, in trusting and believing the declarations and assurances of its leaders and various Arab states. Among the significant examples of Palestinian lack of foresight, mentioned earlier, was the refusal of Jerusalem Arabs to participate in the local municipal government the British had set up during the Mandate. By passing up that opportunity (in order to register their refusal to work with the Jews), they lost valuable lessons in local politics; leaving it to the Jews to gain that experience. Another missed opportunity was Arab rejection of the Partition Plan; so that, when, in May 1948, the Jews established the state of Israel, the Palestinians had no blueprint or any provisions for a possible state of their own. Rather, their trust in the neighboring Arab states' vaunted military might led them to largely rely on these states to prevent the creation of the Jewish state, and in 1967 and 1973, to defeat it: in every case, with the same familiar results.[34] However, in fairness to the Arab states, it must be remembered that they repeatedly fought Israel—at great human and territorial cost to them—in order to give Palestine to the Palestinians, whom they considered—as the Palestinians themselves did—to be legally and morally entitled to that territory.

So far I have sketched the highlights of Arab feelings and attitudes and presented my own evaluation of British policy in relation to Palestine from 1917 on, in an attempt to trace the crucial role played by Britain in the creation of the Palestine Problem. I shall now turn to the role of the United States in Israel's creation and its continuous military and economic support for it since then. That fundamental role, together with Israel's occupation of the West Bank, Gaza Strip, and East Jerusalem in 1967, and its refusal, until the recent Oslo Accords, to give any part of these territories to the Palestinians, are crucial for an understanding of Arab attitudes toward both countries, especially in relation to Palestinian and other Arab (also Iranian) terrorism during the past several decades, against Israelis and Americans, and Israeli and American interests worldwide.

The role of the United States in the creation of the state of Israel and the support it has given the new country since then is familiar and needs no elaboration. It is commonplace that President Truman *de facto* recognized the new state minutes after it proclaimed independence on May 15, 1948; and that the amount of economic and military aid provided to it has consistently been the largest (until recently, $3 billion a year) given to any foreign country. Perhaps less known is the role of the Truman administration in the passage of the UN Partition Resolution of November 29, 1947, in the pressure it applied on several reluctant Latin American countries, which were concerned about the status of Jerusalem. Even less generally known, I think, is the long-standing American sympathy for the "redemption of Zion." Groisser observes how the Bible's influence on Christian thinking led American Christians and Jews to give their support for "'the redemption of Zion' even before the present-day Zionist movement was established in 1897."[35] Presidents William McKinley, Theodore Roosevelt, and William Taft also expressed sympathy "for the idea of reestablishing Palestine as a homeland for the Jews" shortly after the Zionist movement was organized.[36]

These facts, particularly U.S. military aid to Israel, which helped make possible the Arabs' humiliating defeats in the 1956, 1967, and 1973 wars, and which until recently,[37] the Arabs have tended to regard as proof positive for the absence of American fairness or evenhandedness in its Middle East policy. They, and the steadfast refusal of successive American administrations (in full agreement with the hard line Israeli position) to contemplate the idea of a Palestinian state in the occupied territories, have been among the fundamental reasons for Arab anger at, and frustration with, American foreign policy, and have made American interests worldwide a prime target of international Arab terrorism. In fact, the Arab masses throughout the Middle East have looked upon Israel as nothing but a tool of American imperialism, a thorn thrust by America in the side of the Arabs for its own economic and strategic benefit; with callous indifference to its cost to the entire region in terms of oppression, continual humiliation, suffering, rootlessness, economic deprivation, and social and political upheaval and instability.

I finally turn to Israel and its role or share of responsibility for the sorry state of affairs that is the Palestine Problem and the Arab-Israeli conflict as a whole.

The first thing to note is that Israel's crucial role essentially begins in 1967, with its occupation of the West Bank, Gaza Strip, and East Jerusalem, and continues to the present day, with only very partial and limited Palestinian autonomy to date. The list of Israeli military ruthlessness and oppression of the Palestinians is long and painfully familiar to all those who watch television or read the papers, and not only during the Palestinian intifada in 1988. Only a few of the most glaring examples will be mentioned. They have included the violation of the most basic moral (e.g., human) and civil rights of the Palestinian population in Israel's periodic closings of their schools and colleges; the illegal deportations; the relentless building of Jewish settlements in the occupied territories, intended to create "facts on the ground," in direct defiance of the UN and U.S. policy and Palestinian desperation; the bone shattering beating and shooting of "stone children"; the blowing up or bulldozing of houses of actual or suspected Palestinian terrorists, and others who resist the occupation; the imprisonment without trial of Palestinian dissidents; the invasion of Lebanon in 1982, and the regular bombing of villages in southern Lebanon harboring, or believed to be harboring, Hezbollah guerrillas fighting Israel's occupation of the "security zone" in southern Lebanon. To these must be added Israeli clandestine counter-terrorist measures outside Israel, which have resulted in the assassination of leading PLO and other leading Palestinian figures, as well as the spiritual leader of the Shi'ites in southern Lebanon.

These and other forms of oppression and brutality did not stop even as the peace talks between Palestinians and Israelis were going in the early 1990s. For instance, in the Introduction to a publication entitled *The Price of Peace, The Toll of the Peace Process on Palestinians in the Occupied Territories, 1 Nov 1991–15 Feb 1992*,[38] which appeared after the Madrid peace talks, the authors mention Israel's continued "seizure of land, uprooting of trees, and construction of housing, commercial zones and roads for settlers."[39] The rest of the booklet detailed "Israeli Policies Against the Palestinian Civilian Population," which included the number of Palestinians killed or injured by the Israeli army and settlers since the beginning of the intifada; arrest raids and torture in detention; curfew and other movement restrictions; expulsions; interference with Palestinian education; taxation causing "extreme financial hardship for Palestinians"; uprooting of trees, demolitions, and house sealings. It went on to describe Israeli land seizure and settlement of specific parts of the occupied territories since the start of the Madrid conference; "settler violence in the occupied territories"; and, finally, "media disinformation." In addition, the appendixes listed the tax raids, sanctions against land and agriculture, and house demolitions and sealings.

The above-mentioned facts, both relating to the period before and after the start of the 1991 peace talks, help to dramatize some of the specific reasons for Palestinian resistance to Israel since 1967, including various forms of civil disobedience, terrorism, and the more recent uprising or *Intifada*.

The first real turn to detente between Israelis and Arabs came with the Israeli-Egyptian peace treaty in 1979,[40] followed by the Israel-PLO Oslo Declaration of Principles in 1993,[41] and the beginnings of the transitional stage of Palestinian autonomy in the occupied territories in 1994. Later that year came the signing of a peace treaty between Israel and Jordan. But the peace process between Israel and the Palestinians stalled and almost died with the assassination of Israeli prime minister Itzhak Rabin and, especially, with the election of the Likud government of Benjamin Netanyahu in 1996. It was briefly revived, thanks to the efforts of the Clinton administration, in the Wye River Agreement of October 1998 between Netanyahu and Arafat. A month later, Israel began the pull-out from the first 2% of the total of 13% of the West Bank stipulated by that Agreement, in the face of stiff opposition from the Israeli hardliners in the Knesset and the Jewish West Bank settlers, who following foreign minister Ariel Sharon's advice, have been trying since to "grab" as much of the West Bank hilltops as they could before it became Palestinian territory. Since then, Netanyahu has refused to redeploy any more troops from the West Bank, citing Palestinian violations of a number of the agreement's terms. Soon after that the Netanyahu government was brought down by the opposition in the Knesset. New elections were set for May 1999: at the very time when the final settlement negotiations of the Oslo Accords were supposed to begin!

Assuming that the new elections will lead Israel to see its way clear to full compliance with the Wye Agreement, it will enter the final settlement negotiations with the Palestinians in control of the greater part of the West Bank; that is, about 58% of the West Bank and Gaza Strip territory. (The entire West Bank and Gaza Strip constitutes only 25% of the former territory of Palestine.)

To sum up. The chapter set the stage for this book as a whole by trying to do two main things: first, provide a concise historical sketch of the Palestine Problem, including Palestinian and other Arab perceptions or beliefs regarding what Palestinians consider to be the grievous injustices they have suffered in this century; and second, assessing the extent to which these perceptions or beliefs are morally and legally as well as historically justified. With these aims in view, it presented the highlights of the Palestine Problem and the Arab-Israeli conflict from its beginnings, starting with the Balfour Declaration and the earlier Sykes-Picot Agreement between Britain and France, which the Arabs perceived as a betrayal of Britain's promise to grant independence not only to Mesopotamia and Syria but also to Palestine, if the Arabs supported the British war effort by rebelling against Turkey. It briefly recounted the growing tensions and conflicts between the Palestinians, Jews, and British during the British Mandate, particularly during World War II, and Britain's unsuccessful efforts to resolve the conflicts which, in 1947, ended with its handing the Palestine Problem over to the United Nations for resolution. The account referred to, and comments on, the string of wars between the Arabs and Israel that, for a quarter of a century, followed the Arabs' rejection of the UN Partition Plan and Israel's declaration of independence, together with Palestinian and other Arab resistance to Israel, which included terrorism and the intifada after Israel's conquest of the West Bank, Gaza Strip, and East Jerusalem in the 1967 war. The account was brought up to the present with brief discussions of the 1979 Israeli-Egyptian peace treaty that marked the beginning of reconciliation between the Arabs and Israel; the 1993 Israeli-Palestinian Oslo Accords and the subsequent limited Palestinian autonomy; the 1994 Israeli-Jordanian peace treaty; and, finally, the 1998 Wye Agreement between Israel and the PLO. A description of Arab attitudes toward the United States' role in the creation of Israel and the support it has given it since then, and Israel's share of responsibility for the Palestine Problem and the Arab-Israeli conflict as a whole, concluded the chapter.

Notes

1. It is unfortunate that the PLO equates Palestinians with Arabs indigenous to Palestine, excluding non-Arabs whose ancestors settled in Palestine decades or centuries ago. That ought to be remedied in any future Palestinian state, to allow non-Arabs full participation in a democratic governance of the country.

2. See, for example, my "Criteria of Territorial Rights of Peoples and Nations," in *The Territorial Rights of Nations and Peoples*, John R. Jacobson, ed. (Lewiston, NY, 1989), 47–51. See also chapter 3, and *The Morality of Terrorism* (New York, 1998), Appendix.

3. Philip L. Groisser, *The United States and The Middle East* (Albany, N.Y., 1982), 117–118. My italics.

4. Ibid., 118.

5. It should be noted that my criticism, on moral grounds, of British policy with regard to, for example, the Balfour Declaration and the Sykes-Picot agreement, rests on a view known as "political moralism," which maintains (*contra* "political realism" or *Realpolitik*) that moral evaluation is meaningful in and applicable to international relations (see chapter 3). Similarly with my moral evaluation of the Arab-Israeli wars. Just War theory, appealed to throughout this book, is, of course, a major application of political moralism.

    The following passage by Jukka Nevakivi is noteworthy in this connection: "For the United States government and public opinion the failure of an ideal settlement in Syria seemed to provide a spectacular example of a lack of sincerity among their European allies. According to the evidence given by Robert Lansing [on 20 August 1919], Syria was one of the few cases over which President Wilson threatened to withdraw from the whole settlement and to refuse American membership of the League of Nations." (*Britain, France and the Middle East, 1914–1920*. London, 1969, 260.)

    For trenchant criticism of political realism and defense of political moralism, see Douglas Lackey, *The Ethics of War and Peace*, chapter 1; Richard Wasserstrom, "On the Morality of War: A Preliminary Inquiry," *War and Morality*, Richard Wasserstrom, ed., 78ff.; and Robert L. Simon, "Troubled Waters: Global Justice and Ocean Resources," *Earthbound*, Tom Regan, ed., 179–213.

6. However, the phrase "foreign group" is too strong; since, as noted, there was a continuous Jewish presence in Palestine during the two centuries of the Jewish Diaspora, and since the Jews had been the indigenous inhabitants of the land, and had their own state, for a thousand years, long before the Arab conquest. I leave aside the moot question of whether the Palestinians who inhabited the country at the time of the Arab conquest were descendants of the Philistines, who lived in parts of it before Abraham.

7. *The Question of* Palestine (New York, 1980), 15–16.

8. Ibid., 16.

9   In *A History of Jerusalem, One City, Three Faiths* (London, 1996), the historian Karen Alexander notes that "[some] Palestinians claim that there is absolutely no archeological evidence for the Jewish kingdom founded by King David and that no trace of Solomon's Temple has been found. The Kingdom of Israel is not mentioned in any contemporary text but only in the Bible. It is quite likely, therefore, that it is merely a "myth" (Introduction, xvii). It goes without saying that that is not Alexander's view. See ibid., chapter 2ff.

10 As described by Adam M. Garfinkle in "Genesis," *The Arab-Israeli Conflict: Perspectives*, Alvin Z. Rubenstein, ed. (New York, 1984): during the war the British had promised the Sherif of Mecca, Emir Hussein ibn Ali, that the Arabs would be granted political independence if they revolted against the Turks. The deal was made in 1915, "in which Britain recognized and supported 'the independence of the Arabs in all regions within the limits demanded by the Sherif (namely, the entire Arab rectangle, including Syria, Arabia and Mesopotamia),' with the exception of 'portions of Syria lying to the West of the districts of Damascus, Homs, Hama and Aleppo.' Depending on the meaning of "Syria" as a geographical designation, this exception could include Palestine, as the British later held, or it could not, as the Hashemites later argued. . . .The Arab Revolt, led by Hussein's second son, Faisal, and T. E. Lawrence (Lawrence of Arabia), caused the Turks much trouble, and when the dust settled in 1918, Faisal and a ragtag Bedouin army were ensconced in Damascus with British aid" (ibid., 19).

The French wanted to control the area and were promised as much by the British in the secret Sykes-Picot Agreement, May 15–16, 1916. "The agreement defined areas of British and French control as well as spheres of interest and the division of Ottoman Empire territories under the League of Nations Mandate system generally followed its terms" (*Arab-Israeli Conflict and Conciliation, A Documentary History*, Bernard Reich, ed. [Westport, Conn., 1995], 26). In 1919, although Faisal was able to get the support of the Zionists against the French and a "treaty" of cooperation was agreed upon, the Zionists decided not to oppose the wishes of the British. These included French domination in Damascus "in return for British control of Palestine. Thus, the alliance between Faisal and Weizmann was short-lived" (Garfinkle, op cit.,19–20).

The Sykes-Picot Agreement of 1916 was followed, on 7 November 1918, by another Anglo-French Declaration. It stated in part that Britain's and France's objective in fighting in the east the war started by the Germans, was the "complete and definite emancipation of the peoples" so long oppressed by the Turks and the establishment of "national authority from the initiative and free choice of the indigenous populations" (Nevakivi, op cit., 265).

In "Aide-Memoire in regard to the Occupation of Syria, Palestine, and Mesopotamia pending the Decision in regard to Mandates," article 6, in part, states: "The territories occupied by British troops will then be Palestine, defined in accordance with its ancient boundaries"; while article 7, in part, states: "The British government are prepared at any time to discuss the boundaries between Palestine and Syria" (ibid., Appendix C).

Finally, in summarizing the situation, Nevakivi comments that the Arab Middle East "was the area where the allied declarations of peace principles and their enactment came into most upsetting conflict. . . .The entente [between Britain and France] resulted in a partition of interests, in the manner of the worst pre-war imperialism," damaging the reputation of both Britain and France in the Arab world. He adds that, in Europe, World War II swept away a great deal of the resentment that arose over the peace-making of France and Britain, but that "it still survives" in the east (ibid., 260).

11 *The Arabs* (New York, 1965), 274–284.

12 Ibid., 276.

13 Chapter 15, "The Arab Revolt," 274–284.

14 Ibid., 277–278. My italics.

15 Ibid., 280.

16 Edited by Rubinstein (New York, 1984).

17 Adam M. Garfinkle, "Genesis," ibid.,18. In describing Hussein's deal with the British in 1915, the author states that the British excluded "portions of Syria lying to the West of the districts of Damascus, Homs, Hama and Aleppo" from the "entire Arab rectangle, including Syria, Arabia and Mesopotamia"(ibid., 19), which it promised to the Arabs. But I cannot see how he adds that, "depending on the meaning of 'Syria' as a geographical designation, this exception could include Palestine," since Lebanon, not Palestine, was (and is) west of the then "districts of Damascus, Homs, Hama and Aleppo." Since biblical times, Palestine has always been geographically *south* of these designated districts.

18 The interested reader is referred to Appendix A, "The Anglo-French Agreement of 1916," in Aaron S. Kleiman, *Foundations of British Policy in the Arab World* (Baltimore, 1970), 261–263, and Appendixes B and C, "The Anglo-French Declaration of 7 November 1918" and "Aide-Memoire in regard to the Occupation of Syria, Palestine, and Mesopotamia pending the Decision in regard to Mandates," Nevakivi, op cit., 265–266.

19 However, as we shall see later, Britain did make several serious attempts to resolve the Palestine Problem.

20 Ibid., 332–333.

21 In "Diasporas and Communal Conflicts in Divided Societies: The Case of Palestine Under the British Mandate," *Modern Diasporas, In International Politics* (London, 1986), 301, Dan Horowitz gives the following Table for the population increase in Palestine from 1922 to 1945:

"Jewish Population		Non-Jewish Population	Total Population
1922	83,790	668,258	752,048
1945	554,329	1,255,708	1,810,037
% Growth 1922–45	569%	87%	140%

Calculated on the basis of Gertz, 46–97."

22 Their disagreements and disunity regarding political means and ends, and their innocence of the art of political compromise (a weakness that lasted until very recently), scuttled British attempts in 1922 to hold general elections for a legislative council, with a view to leading Palestine toward independence, as the League of Nations mandated. The council was to be apportioned according to religious affiliation—Muslims, Jewish, and Christian. The Palestinian Arab nationalists rejected this and other proposals because they were thought to legitimize a Zionist political share in the governing of Palestine. "They also forced Arab members to withdraw from other British-devised advisory councils, foiling all early attempts made by the British to create a basis for communal power sharing" (Garfinkle, op cit., 22). "The Palestinians insisted on the formation of a national government based on simple majority rule, an arrangement that would have entirely favored the Arabs," and on "the abolition of the principle of Jewish national home" (ibid.), "an end to Jewish immigration, a return to Ottoman as opposed to British law, and demanded that Palestine not be separated from neighboring Arab states."

Arab demands remained remarkably constant and uncompromising through the entire mandatory period (1920–1948). "The only real difference of importance was that while, in the 1920s, the Arabs imagined that they might expel the Zionist settlements from Palestine entirely, by the late 1930s and 1940s they strove to minimize the growing size and strength of the Yishuv and prevent Jewish political autonomy" (ibid.).

23 This point was made a few years ago by Dr. Tantawi, a member of the Jordanian delegation to the Arab-Israeli Peace Conference in Washington, D.C., in an address given at the University of Wisconsin-Milwaukee. Dr. Tantawi did not explain why, in that case, Jordan attacked Israel alongside Iraq, Syria, and Egypt. An obvious explanation was its fear of being branded a friend of Israel and a traitor to the Palestinian-Arab cause.

24 Garfinkle, "Genesis," 29.

25 Ibid.

26 Ibid., 31–32.

27 Ibid., 32. The Peel White Paper (June 22, 1937) The Paper proposed the partition of Palestine into an Arab and a Jewish States. The partition would be "subject to the overriding necessity of keeping the sanctity of Jerusalem and Bethlehem inviolate and of ensuring free and safe access to them for all the world." The protection of the Holy Places would be "a permanent trust, unique in its character and purpose, and not contemplated by Article 22 of the Covenant of the League of Nations" (Reich, op cit., 48). Thus "a new Mandate for the Holy Places should be instituted" (ibid., 47).

28 "This plan proposed an intricate scheme for transforming the mandate into a United Nations trusteeship and divided Palestine not into separate Jewish and Arab sovereignties, but provinces. The Negev desert and Jerusalem were to remain in British hands. The Jewish "province" in this plan was roughly 17 percent of the country," smaller than provided by the proposal of the Peel Commission. "The Plan did provide, however, for the entry of 100,000 Jewish refugees into

Palestine within a year, if the plan were put into action" (Garfinkle, op cit., 35–36).

29 Ibid., 36.

30 Ibid., 37.

31 The classic example before Saddam Hussein was, of course, Jamal Abdel-Nasser's confrontation with Israel, which, together with Jordan's unfortunate involvement, led to the catastrophic 1967 Six Day War and cost the Palestinians and Jordan the West Bank, Gaza Strip, and East Jerusalem. (See also chapter 5.)

32 Although, once it started, it enjoyed the PLO's blessing and support.

33 For the crucial differences between freedom fighting and terrorism, see my *The Morality of Terrorism, passim*.

34 The sound defeat of the Arab armies that attacked the new state in 1948 was by any means solely due to the corruption or ineptitude of some of the Arab commands. The small, British trained Jordanian army fought well.
    In *The Road Not Taken, Early Arab-Israeli Negotiations* (Oxford, 1991), 46, Itamar Rabinovich gives the following account: "The fierce and costly fighting with the Jordanian Arab Legion (in the area of Jerusalem and in Latrun) tended to obscure the fact that the legion operated in those parts of the country that had been allocated in November 1947 to the Arab state or, at least, were not allocated to the Jewish state (Jerusalem). Had Abdullah's army turned during the war's early weeks against the core area of the Jewish state, it would have seriously exacerbated the existential challenge to the Israelis."

35 Ibid., 156.

36 Ibid.

37 That is, with the notable exception of Presidents Bush's and Clinton's roles in helping to make possible Palestinian-Israeli rapprochement during the Rabin-Perez administrations, and partial Palestinian autonomy. Of course, the "rejectionist" Arabs continue to regard the United States as the Arabs' greatest enemy and reject the Oslo Accords and the more recent Wye Agreement. (See especially chapter 4.)

38 The Jerusalem Media and Communication Centre, East Jerusalem, February 1992.

39 Ibid., 1.

40 The most important provisions of the treaty were (1) the termination of the state of war and the establishment of peace between the two countries; (2) Israel's return of the Sinai to Egypt; and (3) "upon completion of the interim withdrawal, . . . the parties will establish normal and friendly relations" (*Arab-Israeli Conflict and Conciliation, A Documentary History*, Bernard Reich, ed. [Westport, Conn., 1995], 156).

41 "*The Declaration of Principles (DOP) negotiated and agreed to by Israel and the PLO in Oslo, Norway in the spring and summer of 1993 was signed* . . . *on September 13, 1993* (Reich, op cit., 230. Italics in original). Their central aim was to "establish a Palestinian Interim Self-Government Authority, . . . for the Palestinian people in the West Bank and the Gaza Strip, for a transitional period not exceeding five years, leading to a permanent settlement based on Security Council Resolutions 242 and 338" (ibid., 231). "Permanent status negotiations will commence as soon as possible, but not later than the beginning of the third year of the interim period, between the Government of Israel and the Palestinian people representatives. . . . These negotiations shall cover remaining issues, including: Jerusalem, refugees, settlements, security arrangements, borders, relations and cooperation with other neighbors, and other issues of common interest" (ibid., 232).

Chapter 2

Territorial Rights of Palestinians and Jews

In "Criteria of Territorial Rights of Peoples and Nations,"[1] I distinguished four fundamental moral/legal criteria of territorial rights (or T-criteria) of peoples and nations. The first I called the "first or original settler criterion" (OSC), which I described as "the . . . primary criterion of territoriality, and so[,] the historical basis of all other valid or *bona fide* T-criteria."[2] Further,

> We can in fact say that "original settlement of a land" *defines* the concept of a T-right to a territory. Logically, however, it can be regarded as just one historically very important sub-form of a more general criterion; viz. that a people 'P' or a nation 'N' that has continuously occupied a territory 'T' before another people 'O' or nation 'M,' has a moral and a *de jure* legal right to 'T': a right that 'O' or 'M' either entirely lacks or (whenever the latter has some right to it) has a weaker degree or form than it. We can call this criterion the "Earlier Settler Criterion" or ESC."[3]

With appropriate changes, the starting-point in my justification of OSC in that essay was John Locke's classic conception and justification of personal property in *The Second Treatise on Government*.[4]

The second criterion is what I called the "non-original or "secondary settler criterion" (SSC); while the third criterion may be called the "purchase criterion" (PC). I stated SSC as follows: "A people 'P' that settles a land 'L' when, or after, another settler had vacated it of its own accord or had simply ceased to exist, acquires a moral right to 'L' when it mixes its labor with the land, and socially, culturally, etc., transforms it into a territory in our sense:[5] into its own territory 'T.' "[6]

A country that acquires a moral and legal title to a territory "through its purchase of it from [its] rightful owner; provided that the transaction, on both sides, is entered into freely and voluntarily, and without deceit or fraud,"[7] satisfies the third, "purchase" criterion (or PC).

The fourth criterion consists in a people's acquiring a moral right to a territory it occupies, if it is given to it by the UN, or by a nation-state, e.g., a colonial power that was ruling it, that has the moral and legal authority to do so.[8]

Following a discussion and defense of these criteria in the article alluded to, the relevant ones were applied to the Palestinian-Jewish dispute about the land of Palestine. To that I shall now turn.[9]

It has become belatedly apparent to Americans and the rest of the world that the Palestine Problem involves valid moral territorial claims on *both* sides, Jewish and Arab, not just on one—the Jewish or Israeli—side. Indeed, as the relevant T-criteria I described will, I think, enable us clearly to see the UN Partition Plan, which recognized the validity of the claims of both Jews and Palestinian Arabs to different parts of the territory, was to that extent fair and just. I say "was to that extent fair and just" since, according to the Partition Plan, the considerably larger Arab population was to receive a smaller part of the territory; aside from the fact that the areas allotted to the Palestinians were, on the whole, agriculturally much less productive than the fertile coastal areas, extending from Jaffa and Tel Aviv northward to the Lebanese border, together with the Galilee, earmarked for the Jews. Some areas allotted to the Palestinians, notably the Biblical Judea and Samaria, were at the time largely parched, arid land. The rationale for the way the areas were to be partitioned was demographic.

Not only did the Palestinians have a valid territorial claim on the land: that claim, I shall maintain, was not subsequently invalidated by the Arabs' rejection of the Partition Plan itself and their subsequent engagement in war against Israel. Likewise, as emphasized in chapter 1, the validity of the Jewish territorial claim to *a part* of the territory is not morally affected by the British Government's policies and actions regarding Palestine, from the Balfour Declaration until 1948; or the Truman administration's arm twisting to secure a majority vote for the UN Partition Resolution in November 1947. I shall begin with the Jewish claims, including the radical claim of the Jewish religious fundamentalists to the entire territory. I shall then turn to Palestinian claims.

The basic moral claim to a Jewish state in Palestine essentially rests on the fact that part of that territory was the biblical land of Israel, the one and only homeland of the Jewish people, although the people of Israel were not the country's original settlers. In other words, the claim rests on the Jews' satisfaction of the "secondary settler criterion," SSC. The fact that except for a small minority, Jews did not reside continuously in the territory for close to two thousand years does not diminish or invalidate their territorial rights on criterion SSC. The crucial reason is that Jews did not leave Palestine of their own accord, but were expelled by the Romans. That fact is of central importance in relation to their territorial claims. Had the majority of the Jewish people left of their own free will, the Jewish claim would have lost much if not all of its moral validity. The fact that an Arab majority continuously resided in the territory since 634 A.D., when Palestine was conquered by the forces of the Omayyad Khalid ibn Walid, would have given the latter a decisive moral claim to the entire territory, and against any Jewish moral claims to any part of it as a putative national home, or potential state.

However, the argument that the British promised the Jews a "national home" in Palestine, reaffirming (on criterion SSC) the Jewish people's moral right to a state of their own, is quite problematic. Leaving aside the moot question of whether they did or did not include Palestine in the vague promises they made to Sherif Hussein of Mecca, the British simply lacked the moral or legal authority to promise the Jews a national home in Palestine in the first place, as I argued in chapter 1—whatever the phrase "national home" was intended to mean. (Similarly, the British lacked the moral authority at the time to make territorial promises to the Arabs.) But given the legitimate Jewish claims on criterion SSC, Arab claims to the *entire* territory of Palestine are also invalid.

It has been argued, on what, in my territoriality article, I called the putative "Divine Promise Criterion," or DPC in my territoriality article, that Yahweh promised the Biblical land of Israel to the descendants of Abraham and Isaac. As I wrote in that article: "On that putative criterion [,] a particular land 'L' (usually an ancestral home that the particular people 'P' had somehow lost and subsequently claims) was promised to 'P' by God (Yahweh, Allah,[10] etc.) [,] or by its gods."[11] But as noted there, that putative criterion encounters at least three serious difficulties:

> [a] The problem of the very existence and alleged nature of the particular deity or deities, all too familiar to students of philosophy, e.g., with regard to theism; and
> [b] the problem of the interpretation of the alleged divine message or promise. From a practical standpoint an additional problem [c] is the difficulty of "selling" such a patently religion-based criterion to 'P's' protagonists [in this case the Arabs, who are largely Muslim and believe in Allah, not Yahweh, while a minority are Christian and believe in the God of Christianity] or to a world with numerous religions and sects; or, on the other hand, to countries in which politics and

religion have become long separated or in which so-called secular humanism is the order of the day.[12]

Another untenable argument is based on the claim that the Jews have a right to the whole of Palestine because they made the land (actually, those parts they mainly settled in, especially the coastal areas, the Negev, and the Galilee, "bloom through initiative, hard work and modern technology,"[13] in alleged sharp contrast to the backwardness and tradition-bound Arab majority. The question is whether that difference, assuming that it is true, constitutes a valid moral criterion of territorial rights; whether it gives the Jews a moral title to (a) those parts of Palestine in which the majority of Jews reside, and, especially (b) the country as a whole. I have heard some people answer that question in the affirmative; although it was unclear to me whether they thought "making the land bloom" (MLB) was a sufficient basis for the claim to the land as a whole, or only to a part of it.

MLB is simply not a valid criterion with respect to either (a) or (b), and would not be so even if we were to add that the Arabs' "alleged" relative neglect of the land was, or is, a result not of poverty or ignorance—or of conscious preference for the "old ways"—but of lethargy, laziness, or lack of interest and initiative. Even then its actions or inaction would not rob it of its T-rights. (Compare: my moral and legal right to a house I own is in no way affected by whether or not I make good use of it.)

It might be thought that criterion MLB can be justified on the same grounds as criterion OSC, and, *mutatis mutandis*, on criterion SSC. For as I shall claim in the sequel, part of the moral basis of OSC and SSC is a people's "mixing its labor with the land," and "adding something of its own to it"[14] especially its putting down historical, cultural, and communal roots in it. But that is *not* what MLB presupposes or otherwise involves. To think otherwise is to confuse two distinct states of affairs. The first is the fact that the land provides sustenance. Second, and equally important, that in time, people become so attached to it that it becomes a "fatherland" or "motherland" to them. Anthropologists, for example those whose views Malmberg considers in the book referred to earlier, emphasize the emotional attachment of individuals and groups to the soil, a universal theme of folk literature, art, and religion. In the case of the Jewish people, it is precisely that historical—religious and cultural—attachment to the Biblical land of Israel that, for two millennia, was both the wellspring of their yearning for the gathering in the land of their forefathers, and a main basis for their claim to a share of that land. But the same attachment, and the logically same argument, is equally compelling in the case of the Palestinians, whose roots too have grown deep in that land.

A further implication of criterion MLB is that some people derive greater benefit from their land through their efficiency, initiative, and know-how, than others. But the latter's attachment to the land and the happiness ownership of it brings to them may be just as great as, or even greater, than the former's. As I stated previously, that is as true of the Palestinians as of the Jews.

It should be added that even if criterion MLB were a valid criterion, it could not override criterion OSC or SSC; otherwise any group of immigrants, say, who satisfy MLB, could stake a valid moral claim to an autonomous or independent state of their own within their new home. Indeed, they could make that claim even if they constituted a small minority of its inhabitants. But that, I think, is absurd.

Again, the UN Charter and UN-created international law does not recognize a right of self-determination to minorities. Article 7 of the definition of "aggression" adopted by the UN General Assembly on 14 December 1974 states that "Nothing in this definition [of "aggression"] . . . could in any way prejudice the right to self-determination, freedom, and independence, as derived from the Charter, of peoples forcibly deprived of that right . . . particularly peoples under colonial rule and racist regimes or other forms of alien domination."[15] The definition excludes a minority from the definition of 'a people': "Chapter XI of the United Nations Charter is the Declaration Regarding Non-Self-Governing Territories drafted at San Francisco. It speaks of the obligations of the UN's members to 'peoples who have not yet attained a full measure of self-government' and saw self-government as a sufficient goal for 'the political aspirations of the peoples'."[16] And,

> In its first twenty five years the United Nations developed and codified a new body of international law . . . . One element of the new international law was that: The prohibition of at least systematic government racial discrimination and the right of a people in a given (viable) territory to attain national self-determination have now become principles of international law *jus cogens*.[17]

The Palestinians' moral entitlement to a share in (indeed, to half if not to a little more than half of) the land, rests in my view on the following facts. First, as stated earlier, they have lived continuously in that land since the Arab conquest in the seventh century. Second, they constituted the majority of its population at the time of Israel's creation. To that extent the Palestinians satisfy criterion SSC. I say "to that extent," since SSC would have been fully satisfied had the indigenous people at the time of the Muslim conquest "vacated it of its own accord or had simply ceased to exist." That, of course, did not occur. The Arabs under Caliph Abu Bakr conquered the country and its inhabitants. Since the Jews too acquired the territory that became the "land of Israel" by force of arms against the indigenous Canaanites and Philistines, they too fail fully to satisfy SSC, but satisfy (or fail to satisfy) it in the same degree as the Arabs.

The roughly equal degree in which the disputants satisfy SSC, fortunately enables us to avoid (a) the thorny general question of whether conquest of another's land is ever morally justified, and whether (b) the Israelites' arrival in Canaan "by the end of the thirteenth century" BCE,[18] and the Arab conquest of Palestine, were morally justified. If the answer to (a) turns out to be "Yes," SSC would need to be modified or qualified to allow for morally justifiable conquests.

Whatever the answer to the preceding questions, there is an important third point directly relevant to the Palestinians' territorial claims—this time to their legal claims. I refer of course to the UN Partition Resolution. Equal legal rights were acquired by the Jews at the same time.

As we well know, the actual situation was scarcely as simple and as clear-cut as all this, given Arab rejection of the Partition Plan, their launching the 1948 war, and subsequent attempts to end Israel's existence. Moreover, Islamist Arabs continue to proclaim that "Palestine is Arab." At the same time, the earlier Begin and Shamir administrations, the Jewish settlers in the West Bank and Gaza Strip, and other Jewish fundamentalist rejectionists have consistently proclaimed that the entire country is the Biblical Land of Israel and thus belongs to the Jews. The radical Maier Kahan and his followers also wanted to see the Palestinians "kicked out" of the country, or—as they euphemistically put it—"resettled" in Jordan.

In light of the preceding claims and counterclaims, we need to evaluate some recent arguments and counterarguments put forth in support of the one extreme side or the other. I shall begin with those that are intended to support the radical Jewish/Israeli claims.

The following arguments, made in a recent book by one Joan Peters, are the most extreme ones I have come across in defense of a Zionist-Israeli right to the whole of Palestine—and, apparently, to what is now Jordan as well. The passages I shall quote, taken from a review of the book's thesis in the *Council for the Advancement of Arab-British Understanding Annual Report*, 1985, summarize Peters' claims thus:

The Jews have been in Palestine continuously, while the Palestinian Arabs have not; before the Zionist settlers arrived, Palestine was empty and arid; the British allowed illegal Arab immigrants into Palestine, which swelled the numbers of the indigenous population; the British also unlawfully removed Transjordan from the Palestinian Mandate, thereby greatly diminishing the area of 'the Jewish National Home'; many Arabs in Palestine crowded into the Jewish settled areas, and therefore when they left they were not genuine refugees; the Jews did not displace the Arabs, it was the other way round; anyway, the Palestinian refugees were not driven out in 1948, they left of their own accord; moreover, there was exchange of populations since Arab Jews were driven out by the Arab countries; finally, violence in Palestine over the years was entirely the fault of the Arabs.[19]

To say that the preceding is an ingenious and highly imaginative exercise in the rewriting of history is to terribly understate the matter. For Peters' claims are a tissue of falsehoods and almost grotesque distortions of historical fact. To any Palestinian, who, like the present author and his family, lived in Palestine during the British mandate, and whose ancestors lived there before him or her, they are nothing short of preposterous. Or as the reviewer whose summary of Peters' claims I quoted wrote about her book, they are "an absurd exercise in propaganda of the most partisan kind, propaganda which even a great many Zionists reject." [20]

For our purposes, the special interest of Peters' claims lies in the fact that she implicitly but unsuccessfully tries to appeal to criterion SSC. That is clearly seen in her claim that it is a "bald fact that the Jews are [the] indigenous *people* on that land who never left, but who have continuously stayed on their 'Holy Land' . . .They never abandoned [Palestine] physically, nor did they renounce their claim to their nation—the only continuous claim that exists." [21]

Peters claims that, "according to her 'original demographic study,'" Palestine had no stable Arab population. She describes the land variously as "virtually emptied," "laid waste," and "sackcloth and ashes," and alleges that "'for centuries the non-Jewish, particularly the Muslim, peoples who did inhabit the land had been largely composed of a revolving immigrant population of diverse ethnic origins who could not possibly have constituted a substantial indigenous "Palestine" population.'"[22] This echoes David Ben-Gurion, later Israel's first President, who, in 1917, "made the astonishing suggestion that in a 'historical and moral sense,' Palestine was a country 'without inhabitants.'[23] Because the Jews felt at home there, all other inhabitants of the country were merely the ethnic descendants of various conquerors. Ben-Gurion wished the Arabs well as individuals but was convinced that they had no right at all as a nation."[24] Former Prime Minister Golda Meier also echoed Ben-Gurion when she rhetorically asked: "Who are the Palestinians?", meaning that there is no Palestinian people.

Interestingly, essentially the opposite hypothesis—although its author too speaks of it as if it were a historical fact—but appealing to OSC rather than SSC, is made by Bertha Spafford Vester in support of the Arab claims. On her account, " the Arab-speaking people of Palestine are not to be confused in race or manner of life with the typical Arabs of the Arabian peninsula."[25] Indeed,

> the Arabs of Palestine are Arabs in name but not much so in blood. And just as the claim of the Jews to Palestine as the home of their ancestors is weakened by the fact that so few modern Jews are really of Israelish blood [since, she argues, the Jews are not 'ethnically a distinct and homogeneous race which is descended from people who once had their home' in Palestine] so the claim of the Palestinians to a stake in modern Palestine rests on the basic fact that they are descendants of a people who have always been there. In fact, the Palestinian Arabs are descended from the Israelites (or better, the mixture of Israelites and Canaanites which once filled Palestine), to an even greater degree than the modern Jews can claim descent from that ancient common ancestor. It is a mistake of tragic political import that public opinion, the world over, thinks it only right for Jews to "return" to Palestine, even if at the expense of the "return" of the Palestinian Arabs to a desert, from which in fact they never came.[26]

Mrs. Vester gives no historical evidence for her crucial claim that Palestinian Arabs are descended from a mixture of Israelites and Canaanites: which if true, would give them the right to a "stake in modern Palestine," as she puts it, if not a right to the whole country, on OSC rather than on the weaker, SSC. Moreover, in my own research on the subject, I have not come across any evidence that substantiates—or refutes—her hypothesis. It is interesting that some years ago, *Time* magazine made a similar claim about the origin of the Palestinian Arabs, again without mentioning any evidence.

One final point concerning Peters' claim that "the Palestinian refugees were not driven out in 1948, they left of their own accord." That statement calls for comment, since, for one thing, it relates to a crucial qualification concerning both OSC and SSC; namely, that a people loses its moral right to its territory if it leaves it of its own accord. That the majority of Jews did not leave Palestine of their own accord during the reign of the Emperor Tiberius, is in my view at the heart of the Jewish people's rightful claim to a Jewish state in (part of) Palestine. At the same time, an important part of the radical Jewish view, articulated by Peters, is that the Palestinians lost whatever rights they may have had to any part of the land when many of them left the country in 1948 "of their own accord." Not surprisingly, therefore, Arabs have categorically denied the truth of that allegation. They have correctly maintained that the Palestinian exodus, during and after the 1948 Palestine War, was brought about by widespread fear of the victorious Jewish fighters, precipitated by the latter's massacre, in April 1948, of an entire Arab village, the village of Deir Yassin.[27] But even if that abhorrent act had not been perpetrated, what is crucial here is the Palestinians' absolute conviction, at the time, that the massacre did occur and that similar massacres were very likely to occur.

Whether *any* Palestinians left because their leaders told them to do so, we will probably never know. But as Edward Said states, "against the frequently mentioned proposition—that Palestinians left because they were ordered to by their leaders, . . . —I must say categorically that *no one has produced any evidence of such orders sufficient to produce so vast and final an exodus.*"[28] He adds: "In other words, if we wish to understand why 780,000 Palestinians left in 1948, we must . . . see the exodus as being produced by a relative lack of Palestinian political, organizational response to Zionist effectiveness and, along with that, a psychological mood of failure and terror."[29] Said also notes that an atrocity such as the Deir Yassin massacre "had its effect. But for all its horror, even Deir Yassin was one of many such massacres which began in the immediate post-World War period and which produced conscious Zionist equivalents of American Indian-killers. What probably counted more has been the machinery for keeping the unarmed civilian Palestinians away, once they had moved (in most cases) to avoid the brutalities of war."[30] According to my parents, some residents of the Old City of Jerusalem who fled the city naively believed that their flight would be only temporary; that they would soon return to their homes, convinced that the British never leave a country they have ruled. The Arabic saying was: "The British leave through the door only to return through the window."

Concerning the Deir Yassin massacre and the refugee issue as a whole, Pamela Ann Smith observes in "Palestine and the Palestinians":

> The vast majority of the refugees left after fighting broke out between the Haganah—the underground Jewish army—and Palestinian irregulars, and later, after May 14, 1948, during battles between the Haganah, the Arab Legion (Transjordan), and the armies of Egypt, Syria, and Iraq. Many initially sought safety in Lebanon, Syria, or other parts of Palestine, particularly during the heavy fighting in the Galilee in the Spring of 1948 and after the massacre of 254 villagers in Deir Yasin in April of that year.[31]

A more serious challenge to the Palestinians' moral and legal territorial claims, noted in chapter 1, is the charge that, by their rejection of the Partition Plan, they forever lost the territorial rights the United Nations granted them in 1947. But as I argued there, that is a spurious claim. First, because the Palestinian masses were not given the opportunity to decide for themselves whether to accept or reject the Plan.[32] But second, the Palestinians' moral territorial rights would have remained intact even if the majority of Palestinians had rejected the Plan freely and voluntarily, with full understanding of the probable implications of their action. Not only that: their legal territorial rights too would have remained intact under international law, insofar as the United Nations has continually upheld the Palestinians' right to freedom and self-determination, notwithstanding Arab rejection of the Partition Plan. Nay, even after the 1948 and 1973 wars, which the Arab states themselves waged against Israel. (The 1956 Suez invasion and the 1967 war were putative preemptive self-defensive attacks on Israel's part.)

The United Nations' upholding of the moral and legal rights of the Palestinians to freedom and self-determination is embodied in the Security Council Resolutions 242, 22 November 1967 and 338, 22 October 1973. These resolutions—the first made after the 1967 war, the second, very soon after the 1973 war—clearly demonstrate that the United Nations did not consider the two wars as abrogating the Palestinians' territorial rights. In fact, Resolution 242 explicitly considers Israel's wartime acquisition of the West Bank, Gaza Strip, and the Old City of Jerusalem as inadmissible, and demands its withdrawal from these territories. I quote: "Emphasizing the inadmissibility of the acquisition of territory by war and the need to work for a just and lasting peace in which every State in the area can live in security," the UN demanded, among other things, "withdrawal of Israeli armed forces from territories occupied in the recent [1967] conflict."[33] Resolution 338, which called upon Israel to withdraw from the land occupied in 1967, "in all of its parts," including the West Bank, Gaza Strip, and the Old City of Jerusalem, in accordance with Resolution 242 (1967),[34] is particularly significant for our purposes since Egypt, not Israel, started the 1973 war.

Resolutions 242 and 338 meet the possible objection that even if the Palestinians did not forfeit whatever legal rights they had in Palestine because of their rejection of the Partition Plan, they surely forfeited them by participating, with the Arab states, in attacking Israel in 1948. But the fact that these Resolutions are still in effect explains why Palestinian leaders frequently cite them in demanding that Israel return the territories it occupied in 1967. Now supposing our critic grants that the Arabs continue to this day to have a legal right to what I shall call, with deliberate vagueness, the "return of the occupied territories to them" (whether that means their return to Jordan or to the Palestinians[35]), he or she may nonetheless argue that, as a result of the Arab countries' putative aggression against Israel in 1948, 1967, and 1973, the Palestinians lost whatever *moral* territorial rights they may have originally had; on the earlier-mentioned principle that individuals, groups, or states that commit serious moral wrongs against other individuals, groups, or states thereby forfeit (some or all of ?) their moral rights.

Since the question here is the "fate" of the Palestinians' moral entitlement to a part of Palestine—a right to which, I have argued, they certainly have—the issue narrows down to the relatively minor role of the Palestinian fighters (the "Munadeleen") in the 1948 war; since the 1967 and 1973 wars were fought by the armies of the neighboring Arab states alone, not, or not also, by the Palestinians. As far as the latter are concerned, the issue of aggression boils down to the question whether their participation in the 1948 war actually was or was not aggression.

As noted in chapter 1, the declared position of the Palestinian leaders up to and a considerable time after Israel's creation, was that "Palestine is Arab." As far as they were concerned, their attempt to prevent the creation of Israel was morally justified as an act of collective self-defense against an aggressor attempting to grab a sizeable part of a territory that was rightfully theirs. If that is granted, the 1967 war can be seen as a continuation of that collective self-defense; while the 1973 war would be seen as the Arabs' attempt to regain territory they lost in 1967 in defending their territorial rights violated by Israel's creation. If one accepts this line of argument, it can be further claimed that Israel's occupation of 80% of Palestine as a result of its victorious 1948 war made it imperative for the Arab states to try to regain at least 20% of that territory—territory to which Israel tenaciously clung in defiance of repeated UN resolutions to the contrary.

The argument is seriously flawed in ignoring the territorial rights of the Jews under the UN Partition Plan.

Some champions of the "Palestine is Arab" position may respond that Jewish rights are no more than an entitlement to participate in a democratically constituted government of an independent, unitary Arab-Jewish state: precisely what the Arabs (they might claim) envisioned in 1948.[36] They might add that partition was a fundamentally bad idea, a last ditch but unjust attempt by the UN to end the Palestinian-Jewish conflict by appeasing the Zionists who were agitating for independence, and committing terrorist acts, including the bombing of British government offices in West Jerusalem. Moreover, that the UN compounded the injustice inflicted on the Palestinians by inequitably giving the relatively small Jewish minority of 600,000 (in 1947), who owned only about "six percent of Palestinian arable land," a little over half the territory.[37] In 1996 Yasser Arafat wrote:

> The [UN] General Assembly partitioned what it had no right to divide—an indivisible homeland. When we rejected that decision, our position corresponded to that of the *natural* mother who refused to permit King Solomon to cut her son in two when the unnatural mother claimed the child for herself and agreed to his dismemberment.[38]

Consistent with that position, the PLO proposed in the 1970s the creation of a secular-democratic Arab-Jewish state. In Arafat's words: "We offer them [the Jews] the most generous solution that we might live together in a framework of just peace, in our democratic Palestine."[39] For the Israelis, the proposal has meant one and only one thing: an ominous call for the dismantling and destruction of Israel.[40] Since I shall discuss the Palestinian proposal for a unitary Arab-Israeli state in the next chapter, I shall say no more about it here. Instead, I shall conclude this chapter by offering the mere outline of a defense of my earlier-stated view that the Palestinian people, in addition to—indeed, as a moral condition of—their legal rights, have a moral right to part of Palestine's territory. A rigorous justification of the claim that OSC, ESC, and SSC give a people or nation a moral right to a particular territory, will not be attempted.

The required justification cannot be *simply* inferred, on pain of committing the fallacy of composition, from (a) some conception of *individual* property rights, such as John Locke's theory of a natural right to private property, or from (b) any theory of individual human rights like the one I am drawing on in this book;[41] inasmuch as a people is not just a collection of individuals but also essentially involves a certain kind of human unity resulting from the existence of one or more kinds of disjunctive sets of historical, cultural, and other fundamental ties or relationships binding most or all of the individuals together, giving them a strong sense of collective belonging and identity. Still, as I shall argue, (1) and (2) jointly provide a starting point for the needed justification.

The gist of my argument is that the historical fact of a people's having a homeland, a territory it can call its own, where it can freely forge its own collective life and destiny, is a *condition* for (a) the ability of at least the majority of its people to realize their basic needs, potentialities, and interests fully and effectively, and so, to realize themselves as moral persons.[42] This is particularly true since (b) self-realization necessarily includes an individual's realizing herself as a "self-in-relation"; as a being that is partially defined by her commitments and relationships to her community, country, people, or nation in addition to her family, relatives, and friends. In the absence of a community's, people's, or nation's freedom to fashion its destiny in its own territory, its members cannot hope to actualize themselves to the full as relational, moral selves.[43]

Stating the matter more concretely, the individual *and* her community, people, or nation cannot flourish if that community, people, or nation is economically, socially, politically, and culturally dominated by another people, nation, or state. The freedom necessary for the group's flourishing includes its members' ability to use the resources of the territory to satisfy their basic interests and needs, including creating relevant institutions and practices.

A people's being in possession of the territory in which it moves and has its being, for its own use and for the use of its members and descendants, and their "mixing their labor" with it and "adding something of their own to it," are particularly important here. For with the passage of time, the land becomes an extension of the individual's and the group's very identity and being; or they themselves become an extension of the land. As they put down progressively deeper historical and cultural root in it; as their individual and collective—including ancestral—memories become increasingly interwoven with story of the land; it becomes a growing part of their essence. The "land" becomes a "homeland," and, in so becoming acquires a certain mythic character. (Compare the concept of the "home" or "hearth" in relation to one's house and land, and the nostalgia with which, for example, the Palestinian refugees or some Palestinians residing in the West Bank, East Jerusalem, or Gaza Strip, speak of their, or their fathers' and forefathers', land that is no longer theirs.)

In "The Myth of the Right of Collective Self-Determination,"[44] Richard De George claims that the right of collective self-determination is a myth in the Levi-Straussian sense. He says that "Myths both reveal and hide parts of reality, and serve to make sense of and validate certain actions. They typically form part of a whole, and come in several variations."[45] And "Myths are evaluated by how well they function, which is to explain and justify some phenomenon to those who hold them. . . .Their explanatory and justificatory functions depend on their being accepted and their cohering with a set of other beliefs."[46] But the mythic character of the concept of a "homeland" ("fatherland," "motherland"[47]) should not lead us to think that a people's or a nation's "right to territory" itself is a myth in that or any other sense. Although the concept of a people's or nation's territory tends to become historically transformed into the myth of the "homeland," the moral character of the right to territory is unaffected by that transformation. We can still speak of a moral right to a territory in relation to a land that a particular people or nation considers to be its "homeland," with all the added mythic meanings, connotations, and associations of the word.

To sum up: since the beginning of this century—leaving aside the two thousand-year Jewish claim to the territory as the Biblical Land of Israel—the territorial rights of Palestinians and Jews in Palestine have been a bone of contention between Arabs and Jews. In order to assess the respective rights, the chapter distinguished four general criteria of moral/legal territorial rights of peoples and nations and applied the relevant ones to the Palestinian and Jewish claims. The four criteria are (a) the "primary or original settler criterion" (OSC); (b) the "non-original settler criterion" (SSC); (c) "a people's or country's acquisition of a moral right to a territory it occupies if it is given to it by the UN, or by a nation-state, e.g., a colonial power ruling it, that has the moral and legal authority to do so"; and (d) the "purchase criterion." Utilizing the applicable criteria, (b) and (d), it was argued that both Palestinians and Jews have comparable—perhaps equal or roughly equal— moral and legal territorial claims.

It was noted that the historical basis of the Jews' moral claim to a modern state in Palestine was the Jewish people's satisfaction of criterion SSC, since part of that ancient land was the Biblical Land of Israel: a land from which they were expelled by the Romans in 70 A.D. That claim was reaffirmed by the UN in 1947, which voted to create a Jewish and a Palestinian state by partitioning the territory. The creation of the modern state of Israel, therefore, also satisfied the fourth criterion. But these same criteria also support Palestinian territorial claims: insofar as the Arabs have lived continuously in Palestine since the Arab conquest in the seventh century, and insofar as the 1947 UN Partition Plan gave Palestinians the legal right to their own state in roughly half of Palestine.

Various arguments designed to establish the exclusive territorial rights of one or the other side—in particular, the alleged Jewish right to the whole of Palestine—were next considered and rejected. One such argument was based on the religious claim that God had promised the Biblical Land of Israel to the descendants of Abraham and Isaac; another rested on the fact that the Jews made the country bloom, in contrast to the alleged backwardness and tradition-bound Arab majority. A third argument, by one Joan Peters, boiled down to the historically unfounded attempt to use criterion SSC against the Palestinians by contending that for centuries "the non-Jewish, particularly the Muslim, peoples who did inhabit the land had been largely composed of a revolving immigrant population of diverse ethnic origins who could not possibly have constituted a substantial indigenous 'Palestine.'" A further argument contended that the Palestinians lost whatever rights they may have had to any part of the country, when many of them left it, "of their own accord," during the 1948 war. In reply, it was argued that the majority of those who left had fled out of fear of being killed by Israeli fighters, after they had massacred many of the inhabitants of the Arab village of Deir Yassin in the early days of the 1948 war. The final objection, namely that, in attacking Israel, the Palestinians forfeited the territorial rights granted to them by the UN in 1947, was met by noting that the UN reaffirmed Palestinian rights in Security Council Resolutions 242 (in November 1967) and 338 (in October 1973).

In concluding, the chapter stressed the fundamental importance of a homeland for both Palestinians and Jews as a condition for their self-realization as members of the Palestinian people and the Jewish people, respectively.

Notes

1. In *The Territorial Rights of Nations and Peoples, Studies in World Peace*, vol. 2, John R. Jacobson, ed. (Lewiston, NY, 1989), 29–51.

2. Ibid., 33.

3. Ibid.

4. Ibid., 35.

5. In *Human Territoriality* (The Hague, 1980), the sociologist Torsen Malmberg defines "territory" (as opposed to "location") as "a space-time system." Thus the concept of territory is dynamic "and . . . [is] the basic expression of the social dimension of a type of 'extension of self' in space to create a . . . [personal field] associated with an animal. . . . The territories represent social forces or [personal] fields fixed in space" (ibid, 27). For other definitions or descriptions of "territory" see my territoriality article, 29–30.

6. Ibid., 37.

7. Ibid., 41.

8. Ibid.

9. What follows, with relevant additions and necessary changes, is reproduced from ibid., Section B, "The Palestine Problem," 47-51, together with interpolations from other relevant parts of the article, particularly Section III, "Untenable Putative T-Criteria," 42–45.

10. Thus Palestinian Islamists maintain that Allah has given Palestine to the Palestinians. Consequently, the liberation of the whole of Palestine from Israel, and the destruction of Israel, is "ineluctable" (chapter 4).

    Clearly, if God/Allah exists, He/She cannot have consistently willed the same territory to two groups who claim that He/She willed it exclusively to them!

11. Ibid., 44.

12. Ibid. But as in many Arab countries, "church" and state are not separate in Israel.

13. Ibid., 43.

14. I ignore, as irrelevant for our purposes, Locke's proviso: "leaving [to others] enough and as good," and Robert Nozick's modified Lockean proviso in *State, Anarchy, Utopia*.

15. Quoted from Douglas P. Lackey, *The Ethics of War and Peace* (Englewood Cliffs, NJ, 1989), 35.

16. Sue Rabbit Roff, "The Contemporary International Law of Territorial Rights of Nations and Peoples," Jacobson, op. cit., 6.

Territorial Rights of Palestinians and Jews

17 Ibid., 23–24. Italics in original. Quoted by Roff from Henry J. Richardson, III, "Constitutive Questions in the Negotiation for Namibian Independence," *American Journal of International Law*, vol. 78, 1984, 79.

18 Karen Alexander, *A History of Jerusalem, One City, Three Faiths* (London, 1996), 23.

19 *From Time Immemorial*, 15.

20 Ibid.

21 Ibid.

22 Ibid.

23 Amos Elon, *The Israelis: Founders and Sons* (London and Tel Aviv, 1981), 134. Quoted from Karen Alexander, 369.

24 Alexander, ibid., 369.

25 *Our Jerusalem: An American Family in the Holy City, 1881–1949* (Beirut, 1950), 365.

26 Ibid., 366–367.

27 Concerning the massacre Edward W. Said writes: "In this book [*The Revolt*], Begin describes his terrorism—including the wholesale massacre of innocent women and children—in righteous (and chilling) profusion. He admits of being responsible for the April 1948 massacre of 250 women and children in the Arab village of Deir Yassin." *The Question of Palestine* (New York, 1979), 44. See also ibid., 101.

28 Ibid., 101. Italics in original.

29 Ibid.

30 Ibid., 101–102. See also the rest of page 102.

31 In *Power and Stability in the Middle East*, Berch Berberoglu, ed. (London and Atlantic Highlands, NJ, 1989), 157. Note also Table 9.1, 158–159. On the latter page the author writes that by the end of 1949 an estimated 430,000 Palestinians were housed in refugee camps, while "another 250,000 had managed to find accommodation with friends or relatives, or through charitable institutions."

32 Itamar Rabinovich writes in *The Road Not Taken, Early Arab-Israeli Negotiations*: "In the latter half of the 1940s the [Israeli] diplomatic effort ["to persuade at least some of the Arab states to acquiesce in the establishment of a Jewish state or at least to settle on passive opposition to its formation"] became even more important and urgent. As the moment of decision drew nearer, it became clearer that neither the Palestinian Arab leadership nor any significant sector of the Palestinian Arab society would accept partition and that *in any event the Palestinian Arabs had lost control over their own affairs, in that all the decisions regarding Arab policy in Palestine were being made by the Arab states*" (ibid., 43. My italics).

33 Security Council Resolution 242 Concerning Principles for a Just and Lasting Peace in the Middle East, November 22, 1967. Quoted from Appendix II of *A Compassionate Peace: A Future for Israel, Palestine, and the Middle East*, Revised Edition, Everett Mendelsohn, ed. (New York, 1989), 279.

34 Security Council Resolution 338, October 22, 1973. Ibid., 280.

35 Note that neither Resolution 242 nor Resolution 338 speaks of a "Palestinian right to self-determination"; although that is invariably the way Palestinians interpret them. But this complexity is not particularly relevant for our immediate purposes.

36 For the current Islamist position, see chapter 4.

37 Yasser Arafat, "The United Nations Appeal for Peace," *Toward Peace in Palestine*, Second Printing, Hatem I. Hussaini, ed. (Washington, D.C., 1976), 5. According to the author, the Partition Plan granted the Jews 54% of the land (ibid., 6).

38 Ibid., 5-6. Italics in original.

39 Ibid., 17.

40 In an interview after the peace treaty between Egypt and Israel was signed in March 1979, Arafat stated: "I offered a democratic secular state but they [the Israelis] say we wanted to demolish and destroy Israel. We put it aside and said we will establish an independent state in any part of Palestine." ("Face the Nation," CBS-TV, Dec. 3, 1979. Quoted from Shaul Mishal, *The PLO under 'Arafat, Between Gun and Olive Branch* (New Haven, 1986), 53.

41 As presented and defended in Part 2 of *Community and Communitarianism* (New York, 1999).

42 See chapter 1, and *passim*.

43 For the concept of the "encumbered" self, and emphasis on the partially relational character of the self, see, for example, *Liberalism and the Limits of Justice*, Michael J. Sandel, ed. (Cambridge, 1982), *passim*; *Women and Moral Theory*, Eva F. Kittay and Diana T. Meyers, eds. (Lanham, MD, 1987), *passim*; and my *Community and Communitarianism*, Parts II and III.

44 *Issues of Self-Determination* (Aberdeen, Scotland, 1992), 1-7.

45 Abstract, 1.

46 Ibid., 6.

47 Similarly the concept of "home" or "hearth."

Chapter 3

Proposals for Peace between Palestinians and Israel, and The Future of Jerusalem

I

The Future of the West Bank and Gaza Strip
We saw in chapter 2 the very considerable complexity of the moral and legal territorial claims of Arabs and Jews regarding the land of Palestine. These complexities were due to the problems of justly assessing the relative moral weights of two criteria of territorial rights, criteria OSC and SSC, which were satisfied in some degree or other on opposite sides of the Arab-Israeli dispute. I mean, the problem of trying to ascertain whether Palestinians and Jews had, and have, equal moral territorial claims. At this late date, that is mainly a live, even burning, ideological issue for the hardliners on both sides. From what we can tell it is no longer a live practical issue for many Palestinians and other Arabs, as well as the more moderate Israeli Jews. But the matter is morally important, for the reasons noted in chapter 2.

Given those reasons, it may seem that the so-called "second stage" of the Palestinians' response to the UN Partition Plan, touched on in chapter 2, which proposed a secular, democratic unitary Arab-Jewish state, would provide the ideal moral solution to the territorial dispute.

The "first stage" of the Arab/Palestinian response to the events that led up to the Partition Plan and to the Plan itself can be labeled the "rejectionist stage." As that phrase indicates, and as we saw, it was the stage when the Palestinian leadership and the Arab states rejected outright the concept of a Jewish state in any part of Palestine, and envisioned instead a Palestinian state comprising the entire territory—but presumably guaranteeing Jewish and other minority rights. That position is still adhered to by the Islamist fundamentalists, including the members of Hamas and Islamic Jihad, who, *inter alia*, reject the Oslo Accords and call for the "liberation of Palestine." Their position and arguments will be considered in the next chapter.

The so-called "second stage," to which I shall also refer as the "first compromise stage," came into being in the aftermath of the successive military humiliations suffered by the Arabs at the hands of Israel. That first compromise stage was characterized by the Arabs as a just solution of the Palestine Problem. They also perceived it as a major concession to political and military realities, an expression of realism.

Although that proposal too landed on the dust heap of history, it will be instructive to assess its moral and practical strengths and weaknesses.

Someone who has no knowledge of the Arab mind will probably find it incomprehensible, given the time and circumstances in which it was proposed, that such a patently unrealistic scheme could be seriously advanced by the PLO leadership and some of the brightest Arab scholars and intellectuals at the time. It is not unlikely that even its proponents had doubts that it would or could be implemented. In fact, it was rejected out of hand by Israel as nothing more than a plan to dismantle and destroy it; as it eventually was discarded by its own advocates, including Yasser Arafat. It was succeeded by what I shall call the PLO's "second compromise stage"; viz, the demand for a Palestinian state comprising the West Bank, Gaza Strip, and East Jerusalem. The recent Oslo Accords between the Rabin/Perez administrations and the PLO, and Palestinian autonomy in a small part of the West Bank and in the Gaza Strip, is envisaged by the PLO, and the majority of Palestinians, as but a step toward a Palestinian state, with East Jerusalem as its capital.

The explanation for the existence of the "first compromise stage" is not hard to find. For that stage exemplifies a general pattern in the various phases of Palestinian/Arab thinking about the Palestine Problem. I mean the Arabs' almost single-minded focusing on what they considered (and perhaps still consider) to be the *justice* of their cause; consequently their constant reiteration, until the latest compromise position, of the idea that a "just and lasting peace" can only be achieved by the attainment of their territorial rights: in seeming oblivion to the hard political and military realities of the situation.

The difference between international power politics and the demands of morality became painfully and increasingly evident to the Palestinians in the late 1960s and in the 1970s; and with the failure of the 1973 war with Israel, the PLO and the more radical Palestinian organizations; such as George Habash's PFLP, Abu Abbas' PLF, and the PDFLP; increasingly turned to terrorism as, among other things, a way of drawing attention to the Palestinian cause and of destabilizing Israel.[1] But it cannot be stressed too much that violence was essentially forced upon the historically nonviolent and remarkably peaceful Palestinian people by the harsh political and military realities. Palestinian terrorism, and the grassroots freedom fighting known as the intifada, are the products of the intolerable frustrations of a people driven against the wall by military occupation and a world long oblivious to its human and territorial rights. The humanitarian efforts of the UNRWA and of private relief organizations were, for a long time, the only significant exception.

The official Palestinian proposal in the 1970s for a secular, democratic Palestinian-Jewish state, focused on the justice of the Palestinians' claims as well as, to some extent, on the Jews' historical territorial claims. That it paid scant attention to the question of the proposal's practicability is evident from the pages of a collection of essays entitled *Toward Peace in Palestine*,[2] published in 1975, written by a number of prominent Arab activists and intellectuals. The collection included Yasser Arafat's speech to the UN entitled "The United Nations Appeal for Peace." The essays make clear that their authors—including such well-known Palestinian intellectuals as Fayez Sayegh and Edward Said—considered the proposal as providing a "most ethical and just" solution to the Palestine Problem. The writers believed that it gave both Palestinians and Jews that to which they were morally and legally entitled. That is, for example, perfectly clear in Hatem Hussaini's "Toward a Peaceful Solution of the Palestine Conflict";[3] e.g., in the following passages concerning what he called "a new society in Palestine":

> Very few people can argue the morality or the legality of an Israeli state at the expense of the Palestinian people. This is why Israeli leaders avoid this complex issue by simply saying that the Palestinians do not exist.[4]

And,

> Peace must thus be based on the assumption that both the Israeli and Palestinian people must have full and equal rights in the land of Palestine. The two peoples must live as human beings under laws that guarantee them equality and freedom. Thus Jews, Christians and Muslims, Oriental Jews and European Jews, dark skinned Arabs and white skinned Jewish settlers must have equal rights.[5]

> The Palestinian leadership have proposed a partnership with the Jews, an equal sharing of the land. The concept of a secular, democratic State in Palestine where Jews, Christians and Muslims can coexist with equal rights is a most ethical and just solution to the complex, prolonged conflict.[6]

From moral and legal points of view, what is particularly striking about the last passage is the idea of equal rights for Palestinians and Jews in the land, implicit in the proposal for equal sharing of the land. Note again Hussaini's following statement: "In a lasting peace, the Israeli people must have full and equal rights."[7]

In making the preceding proposal, the Palestinian leadership went a long way in recognizing the extent of Jewish territorial rights. The proposal also coincidentally agreed with the assessment of the territorial rights of Palestinians and Jews that I made in my territoriality article (although, as I indicated in chapter 2, I have since become more uncertain about the precise assessment of territorial rights on criteria OSC and SSC).

Hussaini is aware of the practical problems facing the proposal and observes that some people have deemed the concept "impractical and unrealistic."[8] But immediately after he digresses in a most revealing non sequitur by adding "yet very few can argue against the principle itself."[9] More pertinent is the justification that follows these words: "Moreover, this solution is much better than continued conflict, war and suffering. Other more realistic solutions, like dividing the country into two, are not based on real coexistence and true equality and thus would no doubt lead to future conflict and war."[10] Since that is an objection to the latest, present compromise stage in the moderate Palestinian position, I shall leave it to later. But note that near the end of the essay, Hussaini does go along with what he calls the PLO's acceptance of "the establishment of its authority in a part of Palestine, the West Bank and Gaza, in an attempt to give the Palestinians there some form of freedom and human dignity." He goes on to stress that "the concept of a secular, democratic humanist State where Jews, Christians and Muslims can coexist in peace and equality is the most durable and lasting solution."[11]

A suggestion similar to the PLO's one-state proposal was made by a Jewish writer, Norton Mezvinsky, who wrote that,

> the solution of the fundamental problem of the Arab-Israeli conflict is the de-Zionization of the State of Israel. This proposal, which points farther past peaceful destruction of the Zionist state to the establishment of a secular, democratic, multi-racial state, will not solve all the problems for all the people in the Middle East, but it could be one concrete and positive step forward for at least some few millions of people in this troubled area of the world.[12]

The vision of a democratic, secular, nonsectarian state embracing Christians, Muslims, and Jews in a "new Palestine" is morally and humanly admirable. That would be true especially if, as Arafat stated in the aforementioned UN speech, it were peacefully realized, so that not "one drop of either Arab or Jewish blood [was] shed." Or as Said Hammami put it, not by the destruction of the "Zionist state of Israel . . . by violence and force."[13] Such a unitary state would have done greater justice to the moral territorial rights of both Arabs and Jews than the Partition Plan; insofar as, as we saw, these rights cannot be justly translated into precise territorial percentages for Jews and Arabs. It would have been a more satisfactory solution from the economic, political, and social-cultural points of view than partition. The "peace dividend," the benefits of a peaceful end to the Palestine Problem and the Arab-Israeli conflict as a whole, could have been considerable indeed. Still, as we shall see in the next chapter, I believe that a comprehensive Arab-Israeli accord that includes a two-state solution to the Palestine Problem can provide in time a very considerable "peace dividend" to the entire region. Partition is certainly not an optimal solution to territorial problems, and may well create economic problems of its own. The continuing animosities and tensions between India and Pakistan, most ominously dramatized by their very recent (1998) nuclear tests, and between Greeks and Turks in Cyprus, illustrate the potential flaws in that kind of solution in general. Partition would have also created severe economic problems for a tiny country with meager natural resources. But that proposed solution was inescapable because, at the time, it seemed to be the only practicable way out of an untenable situation. (Some of these problems may also arise if the two-state proposal is implemented,[14] making peaceful coexistence, cooperation, and interdependence not just between the two potential states but also—and ultimately more importantly—between the two peoples all the more important.)That is precisely why the kind of fruitful relations I shall describe in chapter 6 are premised on, or presuppose, peace not just between Palestinians and Israelis but also between Israelis and the Arab countries in the region. It therefore presupposes a comprehensive peace between Israel and all its Arab neighbors.

At this point one may wonder—as one often wonders about the historical, and one's personal, "roads not taken"—whether the concept of a "new Palestine" could have been realized at the dawn of this century—perhaps up to and soon after the Balfour Declaration, before the Arabs and Jews came to be locked in seemingly mortal combat. I believe that, for several fundamental reasons, the answer could not but have been "No." On the Jewish side, it suffices to mention two: (a) the Zionist yearning for the ingathering of the Jews scattered in the Diaspora; and (b) their vision of a Jewish state of their own. Indeed, General (Res.) Yehoshafat Harkabi states in "Arab-Israeli Conflict at the Threshold of Negotiations," that "Zionism from its beginnings desired to have Palestine in its entirety."[15] Neither of the foregoing aspirations would have been possible in the kind of Arab-Jewish unitary state envisaged by the PLO in the 1970s.

On the Arab side, one seemingly insuperable obstacle to the creation of such a state was Palestinian insistence that (all) Palestine was Arab. The few times when some understanding between an Arab and a Jewish leader occurred prior to and after 1948, until the Oslo Accords in 1994, ultimately came to nothing. The first attempt at some understanding came in 1919, when Prince Faisal, son of Sherif Hussein of Mecca, attempted to enlist Chaim Weizmann's support against the French with whom he was having problems in Syria stemming from the Sykes-Picot agreement. The attempt resulted in "a 'treaty' of cooperation between the two. But . . . the Zionists chose not to oppose British wishes, and those included French domination in Damascus in return for British control of Palestine. Thus the alliance between Faisal and Weizmann was short-lived."[16] The second, in 1946, was chiefly between Amir (later King) Abdallah of Transjordan and the political department of the Jewish Agency. In *The Road Not Taken*, Itamar Rabinovich mentions that the political department of the Jewish agency "succeeded in reaching understanding with three Arab leaders [Ismail Sidqi, the prime minister of Egypt; the Lebanese Maronite patriarch, and Abdallah], although two of them [the former two] lasted only a short time."[17] Third, in the spring of 1949, between Husni Zaim, Syria's first military dictator, and Israel.[18] Ultimately, of course, nothing came of these contacts and agreements. Rabinovich states that the Israeli writer Avi Shlaim blames Israel for failing to take advantage of Zaim's "constructive proposals" ("on the initiatives taken toward Israel in the spring of 1949 by Husni Zaim").[19]

Shlaim writes that the "fault can be traced directly to that whole school of thought, of which Ben Gurion was the most powerful and short-sighted proponent, which maintained that time was on Israel's side and that Israel could manage perfectly well without peace with the Arab states and without a solution to the Palestinian refugee problem."[20]

What the Oslo Accords have so far achieved, and what they have failed to achieve, will be considered at length in chapter 4.

I suggested earlier that the PLO's vision of a "new Palestine" in the 1970s was not, and is not, a realistic solution to the Palestine Problem. Realistically, the most one could expect, or hope for, after a near century of conflict, is that, if and when a Palestinian state is created alongside Israel, the two states (perhaps together with Jordan) would gradually move toward a confederation, or even form some sort of federation. If that does transpire, it could conceivably create a bridge—perhaps in the latter part of the next century—to the sort of secular, democratic, unitary "new Palestine" discussed earlier. At present, near the end of the twentieth century, the moderate Palestinian vision of a Palestinian state may perhaps become a reality in the final settlement stage of the Oslo Accords. But more of that later.

The idea of a two-state federation has been seriously advocated by some writers, including Noam Chomsky, who advocated "two federated republics with parity." As far back as 1971 he wrote:

> The Jews and the Arabs of the former Palestine claim national rights to the same territory. Each national group demands, with justice, the right of self-government and cultural autonomy. In principle these demands could be reconciled within a federal framework, perhaps in the form of two federated republics with parity.[21]

Chomsky correctly noted that "such a long range program" must overcome "the paralyzing and destructive tendency of people to identify themselves solely, or primarily, as Jews or as Arabs rather than as participants in a common effort—perhaps still remote—to achieve social justice, freedom, and brotherhood—those oldfashioned ideals that are within reach and can be achieved if only the will is there."[22] As the seventeenth century philosopher Spinoza remarked in another context, "all noble things are as difficult as they are rare";[23] and the shining ideal that Chomsky described has yet to be approximated anywhere.

In the case of the Arabs and Jews such an ideal is all the more difficult to approximate, in light of their unfortunate, often tragic association for the greater part of this century. Consequently, I cannot envision Jews and Arabs living in the West Bank, Gaza Strip, and East Jerusalem even beginning to work together to achieve the "old-fashioned ideals" Chomsky referred to, unless and until the Palestinians have their own independent state. I say "in the West Bank, Gaza Strip, and East Jerusalem," because a case can be made that, since Israel's creation, Israeli Jews and Arabs have worked together for social justice, in the Knesset.[24] The fact that even after 50 years Jews and Arabs in Israel have not so far transcended their separate identities as Jews and Arabs, in the kind of common endeavor Chomsky envisages, bespeaks its considerable difficulty.

With a Palestinian state as a major step, and assuming it is followed by a fairly long period of stability and peace in the region during which the two peoples can begin to enjoy the "peace dividend" (chapter 6), such a vision as Chomsky's and the present author's may slowly move closer to realization. The Arabs' and Jews' racial and cultural kinship and long historical association, at the time they lived side by side in remarkable harmony, further strengthens that hope. But although I am doubtful that Jews and Arabs will ever transcend the "tendency to identify themselves solely or primarily as Jews or as Arabs rather than as participants in a common effort . . . to achieve social justice, freedom, and brotherhood," I heartily share Chomsky's ideal with respect to all peoples, races, and ethnic groups on earth, and not only with respect to Arabs and Jews.

A Future Palestinian State

With that I turn to the proposal for a Palestinian state in the Israeli-occupied territories, including East Jerusalem, which I called the "second compromise stage" in the present, standard Palestinian (though not all Arab) thinking on the subject. In April 1970, with vivid memories of the 1967 war, I wrote two essays on the Arab-Israeli conflict. The central thesis of the first essay was that the Arabs must make peace with Israel if they are to regain any part of the territory they lost in the 1967 war; since (contrary to the then-prevailing Arab view) time was on Israel's side. That time was and continues to be on Israel's side has been, of course, amply demonstrated during the 29 years that have elapsed since then. That essay was soon followed by a proposal for a peaceful resolution of the Palestine Problem. But although important milestones toward a comprehensive Arab-Israeli peace have been reached, in the landmark Egyptian-Israeli peace treaty of March 26, 1979, the Oslo Accords of September 13, 1993, and in the Jordanian-Israeli peace treaty of October 26, 1994,[25] real movement toward Palestinian independence and toward peace between Israel on the one hand and Syria and Lebanon on the other hand, have yet to occur.

My 1970 proposal for the resolution of the Palestine Problem maintained that the demands of both peace and justice made it imperative that the occupied territories, including East Jerusalem, be returned to the Palestinians (not to Jordan), and that a Palestinian state be created in these territories, with East Jerusalem as their capital.[26] The proposal entailed the Arabs' formal recognition of Israel's existence in its post-1948, pre-1968 boundaries, and the Palestinians' forging close economic ties with Israel as well as with Jordan. Part of the new relationship would be Israel's granting Jordan access to the Gaza Strip, hence to the Mediterranean Sea.

The proposal of an independent Palestinian state grew out of my sense of the aspirations of ordinary Palestinian men and women in the occupied territories. Further, to the extent that it was practicable—since about its justice there could be no doubt—I saw the proposal as a fundamental way of helping to arrest the growth of Soviet influence in the region: something that was of great interest not only to the United States and other Western powers but also to Israel. The essay noted, in addition, that by virtue of its failure to convince the Arabs of its much-vaunted evenhanded policy, the United States remained the arch-villain in their eyes. Thus its efforts, together with those of Britain, France, and the Soviet Union at the time had little chance of success unless the U.S.'s image in the Arab world was greatly improved. Nothing could enhance her prestige there more than a just and equitable resolution of the Palestine Problem.

Since its creation, Israel has reiterated its security concerns as its first and highest priority. Consequently, the proposal stressed that the creation of the new state should be part of a total package deal that included a peace treaty between Israel's Arab neighbors and it. The former's commitment to ending hostilities I deemed absolutely crucial if Israel was to withdraw in any way from the West Bank and Gaza Strip (at present, from the rest of those territories). That meant, among other things, that through bilateral negotiations with Syria, part or the whole of the Golan Heights had to be returned to it. As added protection for Israel, the proposal suggested that the UN guarantee Israel's borders with the Palestinian state (and I would now add, with Syria and Lebanon) by stationing UN peacekeeping troops there at strategic points. Although the duration of their stay could not be predicted, I suggested that they may be required to stay until conditions between the former adversaries were normalized and there was no danger of the new state's being overrun by any of its neighbors, or of Israel's being attacked by any Arab state or states. UN economic aid to the Palestinian state and stepped-up U.S. aid to Jordan, was also recommended.

To further address Israel's security concerns, I suggest that a relatively small, purely defensive Palestinian military force, not complete demilitarization, should help ensure the state's stability and integrity, without posing any military threat to Israel.[27]

A major concern for both the Palestinians and Israel would be the negotiation of common frontiers between the two countries in the final settlement; but given the realities of the situation as I write, it should be amply clear that the idea of a return to "the frontiers of 1967 with minor and reciprocal adjustment,"[28] suggested in his (1978) article, is anything but "completely realistic" under present circumstances. But I agree that "contact between the West Bank and Gaza Strip could be maintained through guaranteed freedom of access along a specified route or routes. This need not necessarily entail the extra-territorial status of the routes."[29]

In its foreign relations, the Palestinian state is very likely to continue its present close ties with the United States and the European Union, whose generous economic aid to the depressed West Bank and Gaza Strip since the start of autonomy, is a most welcome shot in the arm. Membership in the United Nations and in other international organizations, perhaps including, e.g., an expanded Common Market, etc. (see chapter 6), would also be important. But as Khalidi observes, its closest relations would "naturally be with Arab League members" (and, I hope, by and by, with Israel), covering the "political, economic, commercial, cultural and social fields. But its most intimate relations are likely to be with Jordan."[30]

To the foregoing proposals and suggestions, many of which, with or without qualification, remain pertinent today, I shall now add two others. First, a comprehensive Arab-Israeli peace treaty, of which Palestinian self-determination would be an integral part, should include Israel's withdrawal from its "security zone" in southern Lebanon, hence its termination of all support for the South Lebanese Christian militia. For Israel to agree to do so, it may be necessary for Syrian forces to withdraw from Lebanon, which may not be feasible unless or until the political-military situation in Lebanon is sufficiently stabilized under a stronger Lebanese government. As we shall see in chapter 5, Netanyahu's recent offer of conditional unilateral withdrawal from the security zone, provided certain security measures are guaranteed to it, has not met with Syrian or Lebanese agreement, who insist on Israel's unconditional withdrawal.

The proposal for an independent Palestinian state I made in 1970 stressed the advisability of separating negotiations about the future of the Golan Heights from the settlement of the Palestinian issue as such, not made a necessary condition for it. Similarly Israel's and Syria's withdrawal from Lebanese soil should not be made contingent on the future of the Golan Heights.

However, I now strongly believe that Israeli withdrawal from the Golan Heights, either alone or together with complete Palestinian autonomy if not a Palestinian state, is the key to the resolution of the Israeli-Lebanese dispute concerning the security zone in southern Lebanon. Since I shall consider these matters in some detail in chapter 5, I shall say no more about them here.

An important implication of the foregoing proposal is that a sizable number of post-1967 Palestinian refugees, and a similar number of post-1948 Palestinian refugees from neighboring Arab countries, would be able to make their home in the new state. Although that would not solve the refugee problem as a whole, it would alleviate it to some extent. The rest would have to be permanently resettled in villages and towns in the Arab countries in which they now languish in refugee camps, and be provided with concentrated UN and Western economic and technical aid.

Although the Palestinians who lost their property in 1967 or in 1973, as well as those who lost it in 1948, are no longer entitled to compensation by international law, decency if not morality requires that they be at least partially compensated for their losses. Many of them, or many of their descendants, who are settled in other countries, would be unlikely to return to the new state for good. But even those who are inclined to return to stay may decide otherwise if they receive partial compensation for the property they had lost, reducing somewhat the tiny state's problem of trying to absorb too many returnees.

The Jewish settlers in the West Bank need to be given the choice of either staying under the new rule or of moving back to Israel and being adequately compensated (partly at least by the Arab countries) for their monetary losses.[31] Also, the members of all ethnic and religious minorities without exception need to be granted the right to acquire Palestinian citizenship, and their human and civil rights should be fully protected by the new country's laws. Moreover, the Arab countries would be morally obligated to allow their erstwhile Jewish residents/citizens who were forced to leave as a result of the Arab-Israeli conflict, to return, in the unlikely event that some of them wish to do so. Once agin, decency if not morality demands that those Jews who do not wish to return but who incurred financial losses because of their move, be partially compensated.

The Jewish settlements have been a longstanding obstacle to the resolution of the Arab-Israeli conflict in general and the Palestinian Problem in particular. It is therefore essential that the construction of new settlements be permanently stopped. That, above all, applies to the construction of Jewish housing in East Jerusalem. In response, the Arab countries should end whatever actually remains of their economic boycott of Israel (see chapter 6).

II

A state's legitimacy, externally and internally, is not something that can be gained by force of arms. Israel has won the war: it is here to stay. But although peace between it and two of its neighbors has been established, it continues to be isolated from the Arab and Muslim worlds; and because of the unfortunate historical relations between it and the Arab world, it continues to be seen by many Arabs and Muslims as an outsider and interloper. That, together with the lingering Arab and Muslim view of it as an alien power, essentially transplanted into the Arab/Muslim world by the United States by force of arms, has exacerbated the longtime conflict between the two sides. What is sorely needed is a fundamental change of heart and attitude on both sides. One, on the Israeli government's and the Jewish majority's part, a new sense of their being, psychologically and culturally, part—indeed, an integral part—of a pluralistic economic, political, cultural, and historical entity called the "Middle East," albeit with firm ties to the West. And two, a corresponding change of attitude and heart: the acceptance of Israel as an integral part of the Middle East's complex cultural-historical entity, on the part of the Arab states and peoples. Politically, that translates, among other things, into—for Arabs/Muslims and Israelis, a difficult—shared spirit of conciliation and a willingness to compromise on land.

The two-state proposal—leaving aside for the present the problem of East Jerusalem—which in November 1988 became the official position of the PLO's 19th Palestinian National Council or Parliament, is, at present, the most practicable of the proposals that I have considered as well as the plethora of other proposals that have been advanced by various sides, a few of which will be mentioned in the sequel. As Everett Mendelsohn observes in *A Compassionate Peace, A Future for Israel, Palestine, and the Middle East*,[32] the concept of "land for peace, and, specifically, of a Palestinian state, has been embraced by moderates on both the Arab and Israeli sides during the past decade. In the circumstances, the proposal also comes close to a just resolution of the territorial dispute. True, it is less just than the unitary state resolution or even the UN Partition Plan, since the envisaged Palestinian state would, at best, comprise a mere 25% of the territory of what used to be Palestine. As General (Res.) Yehoshafat Harkabi remarks, "they [Palestinians] can hardly be expected to go down considerably more."[33] At the same time, it would be unrealistic to expect even the most dovish of future Israeli administrations or Israeli Jews, to contemplate Israel's going back to its pre-1967 borders[34] (as Syria, for example, has long demanded), and, even less, to the borders envisaged by the Partition Plan.

Not surprisingly, the Arabs who advanced the concept of a unitary Arab-Jewish state in the 1970s, including the contributors to the volume *Toward Peace in Palestine*, were (and perhaps still are) critical of the two-state solution. For instance, as mentioned earlier, Hatem I. Hussaini wrote in his article: "Other more realistic solutions [than the unitary state solution], like dividing the country into two, are not based on real coexistence and true equality and thus would no doubt lead to future conflict and war."[35] And, the late Fayez Sayegh wrote that "neither an '*exclusionist Jewish State*,' existing in all or part of Palestine at the expense of the deprived Palestinians, nor a *restored Arab Palestine,* in which the nonindigenous Jewish immigrants cannot aspire to have a place, fulfills the requirements of such a vision [a vision which proclaims "*the primacy of the human person over the political-juridical abstraction of statehood*"]. Neither an Arab Palestine from which alien Jews are transported wholesale or 'thrown into the sea,' nor an Israel from which the displaced indigenous Palestinians remain barred and still more are 'tossed into the wilderness,' can fit the description of that vision."[36]

I shall comment on the second criticism first. There is no reason why nonindigenous Jewish immigrants cannot have a place in the Palestinian state as I envisage it, as long as the tiny Palestinian state can absorb them, and if they are willing to live under Palestinian rule rather than reside in Israel. Similarly, as I stated earlier, Jewish minorities, e.g., Jewish settlers in the occupied territories, who wish to remain in their settlements in the new Palestinian state, should be permitted to do so and be granted citizenship if they so desire: just like the members of any other non-Arab minority in the country.[37] The idea of Jews being "transported wholesale or thrown into the sea" is so repugnant as to be unworthy of contemplation by any Palestinian individual or government, just as repugnant as the late Maier Kahan's idea of expelling the Palestinians from the West Bank and Gaza Strip to the neighboring Arab countries (e.g., to Jordan, which hardline Jews consider to be the "real Palestine"). Such an eventuality would be another horrible example of the so-called "ethnic cleansing" recently practiced in Bosnia-Herzegovina, reminiscent of the Nazi holocaust during World War II. The Palestinians in their new state can do not less than what Israel has done for the Arabs in its territory: not toss them into the wilderness but grant them citizenship and (some of) the civil rights that appertain to it, including the opportunity to share in the country's governance.

My response to Dr. Sayegh's criticism also responds, in effect, to Hussaini's criticism that "dividing the country" in the manner stipulated by the two-state proposal would not be "based on real coexistence and true equality," and so would "lead to future conflict and war." Hussaini's prediction that the two-state solution would lead to future conflict and war is, interestingly, reminiscent of the fear of perhaps many Israeli Jews (certainly of the Netanyahu government) that a Palestinian state would become a staging ground for attacks on Israel, just like the recent Hamas terrorist attacks during the present autonomy stage. The following passage from the report of a JCSS Study Group, The Jaffee Center for Strategic Studies, Tel Aviv University, entitled "Israel, The West Bank and Gaza: Toward a Solution,"[38] expresses that concern among others, although it correctly states that the creation of a Palestinian state would be a more acceptable solution to the Palestinians than the status quo, autonomy, annexation, Gaza withdrawal, or Jordanian-Palestinian federation. For Israel itself, the serious risks would include the danger that,

> in the long term, the Palestinian state would attempt to realize the Palestinians' aspirations for Greater Palestine (the "right of return") by terrorism, subversion and/or by catalyzing an Arab war coalition against Israel (the "strategy of stages"). It also projects the danger of Palestinization of Jordan, whereby a Palestinian state on the West Bank would collaborate with Jordan's large Palestinian population to engineer a Palestinian takeover of Jordan and elimination of the Hashemite Dynasty.[39]

The third danger the Report mentions is that "Palestinian extremists would likely opt for terrorism in an effort to prevent the establishment of a Palestinian state."[40] But if the guarantees I have sketched as part of the overall two-state proposal are implemented, they would, I believe, considerably minimize the risks for Israel's security. The most serious risk, attacks on Israel by the neighboring Arab states, would be greatly reduced for at least two main reasons. First, because the aspirations of the majority of Palestinians for a state of their own would have been realized, although admittedly not to the extent they would wish. Only the rejectionist (e.g., Muslim fundamentalist, Islamist) Palestinians and other rejectionist Arabs, who harbor the hope for a Greater Palestine, would be likely to pose a threat. But the likelihood of their "catalyzing an Arab war coalition against Israel" would, I believe, be close to nil, apart from the Arabs' painful memories of their resounding defeat in five wars. Both Egypt and Jordan are firmly on the side of peace with Israel, and Iraq will remain neutralized at least for some time to come. The fact that 1973 was the last war the Arab states fought with Israel[41] shows their realization (if they still needed to realize) that any military action against Israel would be met with their swift defeat. It must also be remembered that Egypt, without whom a ground war against Israel is unthinkable, whose peace with Israel successfully weathered its severest test, during Israel's 1982 invasion of Lebanon by staying in the sidelines, is less likely than ever to break the peace[42]—

if Israel accedes to the Arabs' longtime demand for a Palestinian state! Again, the Arabs' loss of superpower support from the former Soviet Union, coupled with Israel's "special relationship" with the United States, now the world's only superpower, cannot but give pause to all Arab states presently not at peace with Israel. The Soviet Union's demise visibly moved Syria closer to the West, including the United States, during and in the aftermath of the Gulf War. That, together with its enmity for Saddam Hussain, led it to join the UN Coalition against Iraq during the 1991 Gulf War. Finally, Israel's return of part or the whole of the Golan Heights as part of an overall peace settlement with Syria would increase the chances of the latter's cooperation in resolving the Israeli-Palestinian conflict, [43] and increase the prospects for a fairly stable peace in the region.[44]

Again, the idea that a Palestinian state on the West Bank "would collaborate with Jordan's large Palestinian population to engineer a Palestinian takeover of Jordan and the elimination of the Hashemite dynasty," is farfetched for the following reasons. First, there is no evidence that the nonrefugee Palestinian population in Jordan, which has enjoyed decades of economic benefits and political power under the Hashemite dynasty, would jeopardize these benefits by engineering a violent overthrow of the status quo. Anyone foolish enough to think that such a violent change can be successfully brought-off would have to think seriously about the Black September massacre in September 1970, and the expulsion of the Palestinian organizations that were fighting Israel from Jordan. (The Palestinian terrorist organization, Black September, came about as a result of that debacle.) The fate of Palestinians who supported Iraq during the Gulf War also cannot fail to provide grave lessons to any Jordanian Palestinians rash or foolish enough to contemplate overthrowing the government in the country in which they are domiciled. In any event, I cannot see why it would not be possible for those who would prefer Palestinian to Jordanian rule, simply to move to the Palestinian state, by agreement between the latter and Jordan (i.e., with King, Abdallah II, who succeeded to the throne after his father's death).

Palestinian terrorism and subversion emanating from a Palestinian state—specifically, from Hamas and Islamic Jihad—would undoubtedly continue to be a possible danger for Israel, as the Jaffee Report states. But that danger, although impossible completely to prevent, should be sharply reduced if in addition to Israel's own largely effective internal security measures, Palestinian police are properly trained to deal with terrorism, and if an adequate UN peacekeeping force patrols the Palestinian-Israeli borders. These measures should more than satisfy the Report's call for the establishment of "elaborate internal security arrangements in the West Bank following Israel's withdrawal," which it calls "an absolute prerequisite," "as a hedge against the danger that the Palestinians would attempt to invoke terrorism and subversion against Israel."[45]

It should be kept in mind that although terrorism is a moral and human scourge, the magnitude of its evils pales, for both Israelis and Palestinians, in comparison with the moral and human evils of the Israeli occupation; even if we leave aside the great benefits that can and should issue from the realization of Palestinian aspirations for self-determination (chapter 6).

In short, the creation of a Palestinian state, rather than exacerbating the present Arab-Israeli conflict and posing a serious threat to Israel's security, should do the very opposite; particularly if the suggested measures and guarantees, including the proposed UN guaranteed peace treaties, are implemented.

Still, it is no mean task to convince the majority of Israelis—in particular, a future Israeli government—that a Palestinian state would not pose a serious threat to their country's existence. For example, as the Report states at the end of the section on a Palestinian state, "under existing circumstances most Israelis would regard this option as unacceptable, and it is highly unlikely that an Israeli government would contemplate its negotiation and implementation."[46] The Report explains that such negotiations would be widely opposed, in some cases violently, by Israelis who regard any Palestinian state as a threat to Israel's existence. It asserts that the creation of a Palestinian state, which would require the forced removal of Jewish settlements, would add to the divisiveness among Israelis and within the IDF. It adds that Palestinian statehood is "potentially extremely risky" to Israel's security, and is as dangerous for Israeli society "as is annexation," without "extensive transition stages to test Palestinian intentions [which in my view the limited Palestinian autonomy and peace process have, since, at least partially satisfied] and confidence-building measures to improve the regional environment" [which also have been importantly, albeit incompletely, taken with the Israeli-Jordanian peace treaty].[47]

Precisely with a view to such "confidence-building measures to test Palestinian intentions" (in addition to what I said in my above parenthetical remarks), I propose the following: first, that the Arabs lift whatever still remains of the economic boycott of Israel, if and when the construction of all Jewish settlements in progress in the West Bank, and the building of housing in East Jerusalem, is permanently ended. Second, and in the meantime, I think an important confidence-building measure can be taken by the Arabs right now if the Palestinian Authority declares that, once the Palestinian state is created, the Jewish settlers in its territory would be free to stay on, if they chose, or move to Israel with adequate compensation for their material losses. Again, given the present limited Palestinian autonomy, the Israeli public should now be better able to know where the PLO leadership stands on the fundamental issues dividing the two sides.

The Jaffee report concluded: "The talks between the Israelis and the Palestinians are aimed at producing an agreement on self-rule for the Palestinians in the West Bank and Gaza for a five-year interim period. No later than the third year, the two sides would begin talks on the final status of the occupied territories."[48] Since the preceding words were written, limited self-rule has, of course, been achieved; but the talks on the final status of the West Bank and Gaza Strip, which were supposed to begin according to the Oslo Accords, have not yet begun. The election of a new government in Israel has raised Palestinian hopes that the stalled Wye Agreement will be soon implemented, quickly leading up to the final settlement negotiations—and Palestinian statehood. Soon after taking office on July 6, Ehud Barak promised to implement the Wye Agreement. But he is now proposing that "Israel postpone further hand-overs of West Bank land until the two sides move closer to a comprehensive agreement on the many issues that still divide them,"[49] including the "future of Jerusalem, water and permanent borders—not to mention Palestinian statehood."[50] Arafat has rejected Barak's proposal, and wants the overdue Israeli pullback to be carried out 'immediately.'"[51]

In an article in the November 15, 1991, issue of the *Milwaukee Jewish Chronicle*, entitled "'Land for peace' should apply to both sides of Arab-Israeli conflict," Rabbi Irving Greenberg, then president of the National Jewish Center for Learning and Leadership, maintained that "Land for peace . . . should mean that *each side* . . . will give up its claim to some of the land Israel captured in . . .1967."[52]

Greenberg stressed that Israel wants its right to exist to be recognized. It wants its isolation and the hostility toward it to end, so that it may be able to pursue a "peaceful life." He therefore suggested that, "as a sacrificial gesture," Israel could relinquish some of the land that it won in a defensive war. That would indicate that the Palestinians have the "right to live in dignity and security."[53] Consequently, as the Jaffee report did, he proposed Palestinian autonomy, but coupled with trust-building measures on the Palestinians' part. Morever—and this was his central thesis—the Arabs need to "yield" land to Israel to make it clear that they have made an "irreversible move toward peace."[54]

Greenberg's preceding and other suggestions and stipulations are, on the whole, eminently just and reasonable. His vision of "some confederation scheme [between Palestinian land and Israel]," although certainly feasible in the long run, would be, I think, considered premature by the majority of Palestinians and Israelis, if it is intended to follow soon after Palestinian independence. Finally, it is unclear whether, leaving East Jerusalem aside for the moment, the Arabs' "sacrificial gesture" toward Israel would involve agreeing to Israel's keeping part of the West Bank and/or Gaza Strip—including the Jewish settlements there and the so-called "political settlements" along the Jordanian side of the West Bank,[55] or whether Greenberg has in mind Israel's retention of part of the Golan Heights: a territory that satisfies his description of "some of the land Israel captured in the 1967 war." Either way, the Palestinians' and/or Syrians' territorial rights on the criteria put forth in chapter 2 would be violated, in addition to the proposal's being doomed to almost certain rejection by the Palestinians and the Syrians, respectively.

Greenberg also stated that, in order to be brought together in real peace, each side had to take risks by conceding land to the other side. That is perfectly true; but since the Palestinians are entitled in principle to at least half of the territory of Palestine, their claim to what is only a small part of that territory, viz. the West Bank and Gaza Strip, is concession enough and to spare. Perhaps what Greenberg had in mind was that the Arabs should concede that the post-1948 territory of Israel, which is 75% of the total land, is lawfully Israel's.

A further reason, over and above the reasons I gave in chapter 2, for my contention that the Palestinians' claim to what would be no larger than a "postage stamp" state, is more than concession enough, is that, on international law and the UN Charter, all conquered territory must be returned to its antebellum country or people. This holds true even when that territory is lost through a war of aggression (as in the case of Nazi Germany and Japan) rather than in a defensive war. As Douglas Lackey observes, supporters of Israel commonly look on the Israeli actions of 5 June 1967 as anticipatory self-defense against imminent aggression by the neighboring Arab states.[56] But he also convincingly argues that Egypt's Straits of Tiran blockade did not threaten Israel's existence; and although Israel can claim just cause, war might have been averted and 20,000 lives saved had Israel not attacked Egypt. Thus he correctly argues that the Israeli attack violated the *jus ad bellum* proportionality rule.[57]

The proposition that the Israeli attack on Egypt in 1967 was morally unjustified does not entail that, on the Arab side, the war was unequivocally defensive. It cannot be gainsaid that Abdel Nasser's actions constituted clear provocation on international law, and on moral grounds. In their defense the Arab countries that engaged in that war can plausibly argue that *they* had just cause and were fighting a morally justified war, at least insofar as they were defending Arab territory against Israel's attack.

III

The Future of Jerusalem

I finally turn to the thorniest territorial issue and single most serious obstacle to a peaceful settlement of the Arab-Israeli conflict: the fate of East Jerusalem. Because of its especially serious nature, there is, I think, general agreement that the future of Jerusalem should be separately negotiated, after the outstanding vital issues regarding the West Bank and Gaza Strip have been negotiated and agreed upon. From the Palestinian and my own personal point of view, East Jerusalem ought to become part—indeed, the capital—of the Palestinian state. As Walid Khalidi states, "without East Jerusalem there would be no West Bank. It is the navel, the pivotal link between Nablus to the north and Hebron to the south. Together with its Arab suburbs it is the largest Arab urban concentration on the West Bank. . . . It is the site of the holiest Muslim shrines on Palestinian soil. . . . Toward it the Prophet Muhammed journeyed on his mystical flight and from it he ascended to within 'two bow-lengths' of the Throne of God."[58] And so on in the same vein. It should also be remembered that Jerusalem is the holiest site for Palestinian Christians.

However, recognizing Israel's insistence that East Jerusalem is "nonnegotiable," I endorsed in 1970 the 1947 UN General Assembly's resolution to internationalize it.[59] That—and Israel's insistence that Jerusalem is eternally Israeli—remains the Israelis' unshakable position. Nevertheless, it is my hope that Israel may eventually agree to relinquishing East Jerusalem to Palestinian rule, provided that (a) a political and administrative formula can be worked out whereby Jerusalem would remain undivided; so that, among other things, the city would remain open to all religions, but (b) also allow East Jerusalem to become the capital of the Palestinian state; in the same way that West Jerusalem is Israel's capital.[60]

A well-balanced book aptly titled *A Compassionate Peace: A Report Prepared for the American Friends Service Committee*,[61] persuasively argues for the creation of an independent Palestinian state, and makes some suggestions about the future of Jerusalem that, among other things, satisfy conditions (a) and (b) above. The author, Everett Mendelsohn, sagely notes that "What is important is to try to identify where the attitudes of the two sides could conceivably permit some accommodation and where the bedrock imperatives lie."[62] At least with regard to (a), such accommodation appears to be possible; since as he points out, "there is some evidence they [the Arabs] might accept the [Israeli] concept of physically united city."[63] Correctly, in my view, he dismisses the earlier concept of an internationalized city, which would satisfy condition (a), as "no longer thought to be realistic by the major parties."[64] Mendelsohn lays down four important conditions, connected with conditions (a) and (b) above, which he says must be satisfied by the administration of Arab Jerusalem:

1) There is free movement about the entire city.
2) For the Israelis, this freedom is not at the sufferance of an Arab authority.
3) Palestinian residents of East Jerusalem are under Palestinian, not Israeli rule.
4) Jerusalem becomes the capital of both Israel and the West Bank-Gaza Palestinian state.[65]

One solution Mendelsohn considers, which would go some way in satisfying these conditions, is the "borough system" proposed by some Israelis, which might "point the way to a solution. Under it, Jerusalem would be divided into sections, or boroughs, some Palestinian and some Israeli: each would be administered by an authority of its own nationality."[66] The question of "who would ultimately control the entire city, especially its security," would remain; but Mendelsohn believes that "it can be deemphasized by joint Palestinian-Israeli performance of some functions and by the form of linkage between Jerusalem and the contiguous Israeli and Palestinian areas."[67]

It seems to me that the borough system makes sense if, as a condition of returning East Jerusalem to the Arabs, Israel insists—as it will undoubtedly do—on having jurisdiction over the Jewish Quarter and the Temple Mount area. That would constitute the only Jewish borough in East Jerusalem, administered by Israel, alongside the Christian, Muslim, and Armenian Quarters inside the Old City and the Arab part of East Jerusalem outside the walls. The latter parts of East Jerusalem would become Palestinian boroughs. But the borough system would not apply to West Jerusalem, which has been part of Israel since that state's creation, and is predominantly Jewish. Mendelsohn's question: "Who would ultimately control the entire city, especially its security," would therefore not arise. As I observed, the Palestinian police force would control the aforementioned non-Jewish, Old City Quarters, boroughs, and would be responsible for their security;[68] while Israel would control the Jewish Quarter borough in

East Jerusalem. Thus Mendelsohn's fourth condition would be satisfied. For the arrangement I described to be possible, and so, to satisfy Mendelsohn's first and second conditions, there should be free movement from West Jerusalem to East Jerusalem, and vice versa.

The Old City of Jerusalem, a site of "such great importance to communities throughout the world, might be the one part of East Jerusalem that could have an international hand in its administration along with Palestinian and Israeli."[69] If East Jerusalem (with or without the Jewish Quarter, etc.) comes under Palestinian rule, it is unlikely that the Palestinians would accept any "international hand" in the walled city's administration. In any event, such an international hand would not be needed to protect the holy sites in East Jerusalem, provided that the autonomy that Christians, Muslims, and Jews have enjoyed in ecclesiastical matters since Ottoman times, and has been guaranteed by every political administration since, continues in effect in that part of the city.

I think Mendelsohn is correct that free movement between East and West Jerusalem would pose the problem of establishing an effective border control between Israel and the West Bank-Gaza Palestinian entity. He writes: "Unless special steps were taken, anyone entering Jerusalem from either country would be free to cross Jerusalem into the other country. Again, inventive solutions would be required, the most obvious of which would involve special treatment of all traffic into and out of Jerusalem."[70]

Given Israel's great sensitivity to the issue, the idea of Palestinians freely crossing from East Jerusalem into Israel through West Jerusalem would pose a considerable security problem for it. But if Jerusalem as a whole is to be a physically undivided city with free movement for Israelis into East Jerusalem, the Palestinian residents of East Jerusalem should, reciprocally, have access to West Jerusalem, even if not complete freedom of movement at the outset. The main "border problem," as far as Jerusalem vis-a-vis Israel is concerned, would then boil down to the problem of Israel's ability to control in some way those Palestinians who wish to cross into Israel from West Jerusalem, for work or other innocent purposes. The border-checking of special identity cards issued by Israel to Palestinians wishing to travel to other parts of that country, would be one way, similar to Israel's present practice with regard to Palestinians crossing into Israel to work.

I shall conclude with Rabbi Greenberg's wise final words in the article referred to, concerning the disposition of Jerusalem: "Borough arrangements, confederation, legal condominium, open-borders—there are a hundred imaginative ways for exchanging land or legal title. If you will peace, it is no dream." [71]

To sum up. As we saw in chapter 1, the British made a number of unsuccessful efforts to resolve the Palestinian-Jewish-British conflict over the respective territorial rights of Palestinians and Jews during the Mandate. Throughout, and for more than two decades, the unanimous position of the Palestinian leaders was that "Palestine is Arab" and must come under Palestinian rule. Thus they rejected out of hand the idea of a Jewish state in any part of Palestine. This position I called the first, "rejectionist stage" in the Palestinians' (as well as the Arab states') stand vis-à-vis the Jewish territorial claims. Since the creation of the state of Israel in the face of repeated Arab armed resistance, and, particularly, since the total dispossession of the Palestinian people, from 1967 until the 1993 Oslo Accords, a plethora of proposals for the achievement of a just and lasting peace between the Palestinians and Israel, guaranteeing the territorial rights of both sides, have been put forward by concerned political leaders and scholars. The present chapter consisted of an attempt to present and evaluate the most important of the proposals. The first two sections concentrated on proposals concerning the future of the West Bank and Gaza Strip, while the last section focused on the future of Jerusalem.

In the 1970s, the PLO under Yasser Arafat's leadership, replaced the rejectionist position by what I called the "first compromise stage," although the former remains the position of the Palestinian and other Islamists, including the members of Hamas and Palestinian Islamic Jihad. Conceding in their pronouncements and writings that the Jews/Israelis too had valid territorial rights and claims, Arafat and some prominent Arab scholars tried to harmonize the rights of both parties by proposing the creation of a unitary secular-democratic Palestinian-Jewish state. Although that proposal was eminently just and morally and humanly admirable, it unfortunately was utterly unrealistic and impracticable, and Israel quickly rejected it as tantamount to Israel's destruction. What eventually took its place, as the "second compromise stage," is the current "two-state proposal," which calls for the creation of a Palestinian state in the West Bank and Gaza Strip (with East Jerusalem as its capital), alongside Israel. Some writers have gone further by proposing a "two-state federation" between a Palestinian state and Israel.

Although the concept of a Palestinian state in part or the whole of the West Bank and Gaza Strip, with East Jerusalem as its capital, does less justice to Palestinian rights than the earlier one-state proposal, it was defended in this chapter as the natural next stage in the peace process, beyond the present, limited autonomy. It was maintained that with the necessary safeguards for Israel's security, it can bring a stable peace between Palestinians and Israelis. The salient features of such a state of affairs was then described, which included the safeguards that state must possess to ensure Israel's security and other fundamental Israeli concerns. For example, those voiced in the report of a JCSS Study Group at The Jaffe Center for Strategic Studies, Tel Aviv University. Rabbi Irving Greenberg's more positive, conciliatory views, including his statement that each side should "give up its claim to some of the land Israel captured in the 1967 Six-Day War," and his suggestion that "as a sacrificial gesture, Israel could give up land won in a defensive war," as a statement that the Palestinians have the "right to live in dignity and security" was met with approval. But it was not quite clear whether he endorsed the concept of a Palestinian state; although his vision of "some confederation scheme" between Palestinian land and Israel seemed to imply it.

The last section of the chapter was devoted to the thorniest territorial issue and single most important obstacle to a peaceful settlement of the Palestinian/Arab-Israeli conflict: the future of Jerusalem. I think it safe to say that all Arabs and Muslims without exception agree that East Jerusalem must become the capital of the future Palestinian state. Its religious status as the holiest site for both Judaism and Christianity, and the third holiest site for Islam, makes it imperative to resolve its final status separately from negotiations about the final status of the West Bank and Gaza Strip; particularly since Israel has throughout insisted that Jerusalem is indivisible and its status "non-negotiable." Despite that insistence, the hope was expressed that a political and administrative formula can be found whereby Jerusalem would remain undivided, but also allow East Jerusalem to become the capital of the Palestinian state. To that end, various proposals were discussed; most notably the "borough system" proposed by some Israelis and favorably reviewed by Everett Mendelsohn of the American Friends committee. It was agreed that the borough system would go some way in satisfying the important conditions that, according to Mendelsohn, must be satisfied by the administration of Arab Jerusalem. The alternative proposal for the internationalization of Jerusalem, affirmed by the UN in 1948 and 1949, and reaffirmed in 1973, was set aside as no longer a viable option for either Israel or the Palestinians. But the possibility was left open that, as Mendelsohn proposed, the "walled city itself could have an international hand in its administration along with Palestinian and Israeli."[72]

Notes

1. See my *The Morality of Terrorism* (New York, 1988), chapter 2, and *passim*.

2. Hatem I. Hussaini, ed., The Arab Information Center, Washington, D.C. Second Printing, 1976.

3. Ibid., 44–48.

4. Ibid., 44.

5. Ibid., 46.

6. Ibid., 46-47. Cf. Arafat's address, especially 17-18, in relation to the present proposal; and Fayez A. Sayegh's "A Palestinian Vision: A Just Peace—For All," op cit., 49–51. The other authors express similar views.

7. Ibid., 47.

8. Ibid.

9. Ibid.

10. Ibid.

11. Ibid.

12. *Zionism: The Dream and the Reality*, Gary V. Smith, ed. Quoted from *Toward Peace in Palestine*, 56–57.

13. "A Palestinian Strategy for Peaceful Co-Existence," in op cit., 21.

14. One economic problem that may plague a Palestinian state in the West Bank and Gaza Strip is illustrated by the Israeli government's continually punishing the Palestinians in these territories for terrorist violence, by temporarily closing the borders of these territories, even after the recent establishment of partial Palestinian autonomy. The first example of such closings occurred in April 1993. (See, for example, "Territory closing shows Palestinian dependence," with the caption: "It serves as a warning of economic perils of a complete separation." *Milwaukee Journal*, April 26, 1993, A3.)

15. The paper was presented at the Washington Symposium of Americans for Peace Now, October 3, 1991, 6.

16. Garfinkle, "Genesis," 19–20.

17. Oxford, 1991, 43.

18. Ibid., 8, and chapter 3, 65–110.

19. Op cit., 8.

Proposals for Peace between Palestinians and Israel

20 "Husni Zaim and the Plan to Resettle Palestinian Refugees in Syria," *Middle East Focus*, Fall 1986, 26–31. Quoted from Rabinovich, op cit., 9. Shlaim writes that "Zaim regarded peace with Israel and the resettlement of the refugees as essential for the attainment of [social reform and economic development]. . . . During his brief tenure of power [as Syria's first military dictator] he gave Israel every opportunity to bury the hatchet and possibly lay the foundations for peaceful coexistence in the long term. If his overtures were spurned, . . . the fault must be sought not with Zaim but on the Israeli side" (ibid.). For a detailed discussion of this episode, see Rabinovich, chapter 3, "Israel and Husni Zaim."

21 In *The Arab World from Nationalism to Revolution*, Abdeen Jabara, ed. Quoted from Hussaini, *Toward Peace in Palestine*, 53.

22 Ibid.

23 *Ethic*, Part V, Prop. XLII, in Spinoza, *Selections* (New York, 1958), John Wild, ed., 400.

24 But note my remarks about the second-class status of Israeli Arabs in chapter 7.

25 "*The peace treaty comprises thirty articles, . . . The treaty resolved the major outstanding issues between the two parties in the areas of security, border demarcation, water, and the establishment of normalized relations. . . . They will establish peace, full diplomatic and normalized relations. Israel will recognize Jordan's special role with respect to the Muslim holy places in Jerusalem. They will seek economic cooperation as a pillar of peace as noted various areas of potential effort, especially tourism*" (Reich, op cit., 264. Italics in original).

26 In "Thinking the Unthinkable: A Sovereign Palestinian State," *Palestine Reborn* (London. New York, 1992), 82–104. Reprinted from *Foreign Affairs*, vol. 56, No. 4 (July 1978), 695–713, Walid Khalidi eloquently expressed views very similar to the present author. For example, concerning "*The Juridical Status of the Palestine State,*" he writes: "The cornerstone is the concept of Palestinian sovereignty. Not half-sovereignty, or quasi-sovereignty or ersatz sovereignty. But a sovereign, independent Palestinian state. Only such a state would win the endorsement of the PLO. Only such a state is likely to effect a psychological breakthrough with the Palestinians under occupation and in the Diaspora. It would lead them out of political limbo in which they have lingered since 1948. It would end their anonymous ghost-like existence as a non-people. It would terminate their dependence on the mercy, clarity or tolerance of other parties, whether Arab, Israeli or international. It would be a point of reference, a national anchorage, a centre of hope and achievement" (ibid., 88–89).

27 Op cit., 91ff. Khalidi convincingly argues against, on the one hand, a Palestinian state "bristling with the most sophisticated lethal weapons systems" and "a demilitarized state" on the other hand. But he appears to favor a larger national armed forces than I think would be acceptable to Israel, at least in the early years of Palestinian statehood. As regards the task of keeping internal peace, curbing "adventurism across the border into Israel," and protecting the hundreds of thou-

sands of tourists and pilgrims who Khalidi thinks would annually visit the Palestinian state, something like the present police force in the West Bank and Gaza Strip, which is about forty thousand strong, should be quite adequate.

28. Ibid., 89.

29. Ibid.

30. Ibid., 91.

31. If the continual conflicts that have resulted from the 1997 "division" of Gaza City, 80% to 20%, between Palestinians and 500 Jewish settlers, is any indication, it would be unthinkable that any Jewish settlers on the West Bank would opt to live under Palestinian rule—or to leave their settlements for Israel. In the event of Palestinian sovereignty, what appears much more likely is a lot of Israeli tinkering designed to keep all Jewish settlements outside the Palestinian state. Of course, the very idea of Palestinian autonomy, let alone of independence, is utterly repugnant to the settlers (see chapter 4).

32. A Report Prepared for the American Friends Service Committee, Revised Edition (New York, 1989).

33. Harkabi, op cit., 5. In fact, it is very doubtful that the Palestinians will get the entire West Bank and Gaza Strip, even given Barak's recent pronouncements indicating that Israel intends to implement the Wye River Agreement—in sharp contrast to the Netanyahu government's position; for example, then Foreign Minister Ariel Sharon's declaration, on the heels of that agreement, urging Jews to grab as much high ground on the West Bank as they could before the agreement came into effect. The declaration, which was approved by the Israeli Cabinet, was in line with Netanyahu's statements that in the final settlement Israel wants to retain control of the West Bank heights for security reasons.

34. Soon after taking office, Ehud Barak, Israel's new prime minister, publicly ruled that out.

35. Hussaini, op cit., 47.

36. "A Palestinian Vision: A Just Peace—For All," op cit., 50. Italics in original.

37. But see my earlier remarks concerning the Jewish settlers in the West Bank. Particularly significant (and always conflict-laden) is the situation with regard to the religious Jews living in Hebron, protected by the Israeli military. They would certainly never opt or agree to return to Israel.

38. *From the West Bank and Gaza: Israel's Options for Peace*, 1988.

39. Ibid., 12.

40. Ibid.

41. nd, to a much lesser extent, and mainly by proxy, Syria fought against the invading Israeli army in Lebanon in 1982–1983.

Proposals for Peace between Palestinians and Israel 65

42 Unless, of course, the present Egyptian regime is overthrown by Islamic fundamentalists who reject the Egypt-Israel peace treaty. Similarly, *mutatis mutandis*, with Jordan. But an Islamist regime in either country is most unlikely, at least in the foreseeable future.

43 A point stressed in my "Territorial Rights. . .," *passim*. In fact, Barak is contemplating a single, comprehensive peace agreement involving Syria, Lebanon, *and* the Palestinians, rather than bilateral agreements with each of these parties.

44 We must not also forget the awesome power of Israel's atomic arsenal: an obvious reason for Iraq's attempts to develop nuclear, chemical, and biological weapons. During his tenure as Prime Minister of Israel, Menachem Begin more than hinted that his country would use atomic bombs in self-defense, if its survival was threatened; and during the Gulf War Israel was prepared to respond with nuclear weapons, if Iraq used chemical or biological weapons against it.

45 Ibid., 12-13.

46 Ibid., 13. Perhaps awareness of this has led Yasser Arafat to express his determination to declare Palestinian independence in May 1999. However, Arafat recently decided to wait until the year 2000: no doubt largely persuaded by Barak's Labor victory in the recent Israeli elections, and his apparent sympathetic stand with regard to the idea of Palestinian statehood.

47 Ibid.

48 Op cit.

49 *Milwaukee Journal-Sentinel*, July 28, 1999.

50 Ibid.

51 Ibid.

52 Op cit., 4. Italics in original.

53 Ibid.

54 Ibid. Whether or not the Palestinian Authority "yields" any part of the West Bank to Israel in the final settlement of the Palestine Problem, it is clear that Israel plans to permanently keep part or the whole of the approximately 58% of the West Bank it would still occupy after its withdrawal from the 13% of the land required by the Wye Agreement. include the Jewish settlements on the West Bank and Gaza Strip.

55 During the Netanyahu administration, Israel's determination to hold on to the settlements was evidenced by the visit of the Israeli "Finance Minister Yaakov Neeman [who] came here last weekend to request aid to fortify Jewish settlements and build roads that bypass Palestinian towns" (*Milwaukee Journal-Sentinel*, November 26, 1998). More recently, in July 1999, Prime Minister Barak publicly stated that, although no new Jewish settlements will be built on the West Bank, Israel will keep existing ones in the final settlement.

56 Lackey observes that blockades "have traditionally been considered acts of war, and blockades were prominently listed as acts of aggression in the 1977 U.N. definition of aggression.... By this standard, Israeli actions... [were] simple self-defense, not anticipatory self-defense." *The Ethics of War and Peace* (Englewood Cliffs, NJ, 1989), 37.

57 In speaking of the violation of the proportionality rule, we must also not forget the evils of more than 30 years of Israeli occupation of the West Bank, Gaza Strip, and East Jerusalem, which have, directly and indirectly, resulted from the Six Day War. Consequently, Israel must also be held partly responsible for its violation, at least until 1994, of the "just peace" rule.

58 Op cit., 94.

59 In "The Status of Jerusalem Under International Law And United Nations Resolutions," *Economic, Legal, and Demographic Dimensions of Arab-Israeli Relations*, vol. 6, Ian S. Lustick, ed., New York, 1994, Henry Cattan argues that, under international law and United Nations resolutions, "there now exists a fairly general consensus that sovereignty over Jerusalem as an integral part of Palestine was at all times vested in the people of Palestine," both during Turkish times, and since then" (ibid., 54–55). "Although the war of 1948 and the military occupation of Jerusalem prevented the Palestinians from exercising their sovereignty effectively on the termination of the Mandate, their sovereignty was not lost, ... either by reason of the United Nations resolution which internationalized Jerusalem or as a result of its occupation and annexation" (ibid., 55). Again, "the internationalization of Jerusalem was not abrogated by reason of its occupation in 1948 by Israel and Jordan. In fact, such internationalization was reaffirmed by the General Assembly in resolution 194 of December 11, 1948 and resolution 303 of December 9, 1949, significantly *after* Israel's occupation of modern [Western] Jerusalem and Jordan's occupation of the Old City" (ibid., 57. Italics in original). The author's conclusion is that "the legal status of Jerusalem rests upon a special international regime [,] ... which envisages its [the City of Jerusalem's] administration by the United Nations but leaves other attributes of sovereignty, mainly the powers of legislation, taxation and the judiciary, vested in the inhabitants"(ibid., 63).

60 In a *New York Times*, September 22, 1997, article, Thomas Friedman reported that Jerusalem has lately increasingly become a "city of tension.... Palestinians ... now live in fear of arbitrary eviction and secular Israelis feel increasingly alienated by the ultra-Orthodox." He also reported that two years ago secret meetings took place between Abu Mazen, Arafat's deputy, and Yossi Beilin, Shimon Perez's deputy, to work out a "possible final settlement [concerning Jerusalem]," between Israelis and Palestinians. In these meetings, they suggested that the Palestinian village of Abu Dis, which lies just outside Jerusalem's municipal boundaries, "might become the Palestinians' administrative capital." The city would be called 'Al-Quds,'which is the Arabic name for Jerusalem. That would give Palestinians a connection with Jerusalem, and will allow Israelis to claim that Jerusalem "remained unified under their control." Abu Dis is connected to the Old City of Jerusalem through the Arab neighborhood of Ras al-Amud. The settlers moved

in there to prevent the Abu Mazen-Beilin compromise from working. At the same time, the Israeli Ministry of Interior has invoked an old law which states that any Palestinian who has "moved the 'center of his life' away from Jerusalem for an extended period" will lose his ID card.

It is certain that no ordinary Palestinian would ever contemplate, let alone accept, any substitute for East Jerusalem; and I disagree with Friedman that, inescapably, the peace of Jerusalem has to be built on a compromise such as the Abu Mazen-Beilin compromise. I also disagree that Jerusalem should remain the unified capital of Israel (alone). That is not a necessary condition for the Old City's remaining an open city to all religions, as Friedman thinks.

61   Revised edition (New York, 1989).

62   "Notes On Jerusalem," ibid., 125.

63   Ibid., 126.

64   Ibid.

65   Ibid., 129.

66   Ibid.

67   Ibid.

68   But East Jerusalem would be demilitarized, as a special exception to the rest of the Palestinian state. This agrees with Mendelsohn's speculation that "Israel . . . might well insist that military forces of a Palestinian West Bank entity (limited though they might be) should not be brought into Jerusalem. To secure such a limitation, Israel might have to accept a similar restriction on its forces, with the effect of achieving a form of demilitarization of the city in many ways appropriate to its world-wide religious significance" (ibid., 130).

69   Ibid. Compare with Cattan's position in note 58.

70   Ibid., 129–130.

71   Op cit., 4.

72   Mendelsohn, op cit., 129.

Chapter 4

From Autonomy to Independence

"Those who cannot remember the past are condemned to repeat it"
—George Santayana, *The Life of Reason*

I

The promise of full Palestinian autonomy, over the entire West Bank and Gaza Strip, is still unfulfilled, with only a fraction of the territory under limited Palestinian administration, and only partial implementation of the transitional stage of the Oslo Accords, including the Wye Agreement of October 1998. Nonetheless, I believe that Palestinian autonomy is a natural step toward Palestinian statehood, proposed in chapter 3; and which Yasser Arafat hopes to achieve in 1999. Consequently, notwithstanding the plethora of problems Palestinians and Israelis have had to contend with since 1993, autonomy has been, on the whole, a move in the right direction.

As a road to Palestinian independence, autonomy is important in at least two ways. First, it is giving Palestinians a modicum of experience in self-government. Second, it has provided an acid test, for Israel and the world, of the ability of Palestinians to govern themselves, and of the Palestinian Authority's (PNA's) commitment to curb Palestinian terrorism and to coexist peacefully with Israel. To the extent that it has passed these tests, it should convince all but the most radical Israeli rejectionists of the possibility of an orderly, stable, and peaceful Palestinian state. I say this since nothing Palestinians could possibly do would incline the rejectionists to accept the present autonomy, let alone a future Palestinian state.

As we know, the PNA's record to date has been mixed, and has justly incurred criticism not only from the Netanyahu government but also from within the Palestinian Cabinet itself, as well as from ordinary Palestinians who have had the courage (despite actual or threatened punishment) to publicly criticize or protest against the Authority's abuses.[1]

In line with the preceding, the rest of the chapter will be devoted to a qualified defense of the Oslo Accords and Palestinian-Israeli peace process (and, by implication, the Wye Agreement) by, first, responding to the radical Islamist rejectionists' objections to them; and second, by considering ways in which these and radical Israeli rejectionists may be marginalized.

II

Palestinian Islamist Rejectionism

Although a number of the Islamist objections to the Oslo Accords are partly or wholly correct or justified, I shall contend in this section that they fail to (a) impugn the legitimacy of these agreements, and the modest gains that Palestinian autonomy have so far gained from them. Further, (b) these objections do not succeed in negating the political, economic, social—in general, the human—significance of the autonomy for both Palestinians and Israelis; especially as it constitutes an important practical step toward the hoped-for Palestinian state.

The general thrust of my argument is that the objections generally ignore the realities of the Palestinian-Israeli situation, at the time of the negotiations that led to the Accords; and that, had the PLO awaited more favorable conditions to negotiate with Israel, or had insisted on better terms than it was able to get during the exhausting, protracted process; for example, had they held out for nothing less a Palestinian state, with East Jerusalem as its capital, it is certain that no agreement at all would have occurred, and even the idea of partial autonomy would have gone by the board. Indeed, given their radical goal of "liberating" the whole of erstwhile Palestine, the Islamist rejectionists would have been only partly satisfied even if Israel had agreed to the creation of a Palestinian state in the whole of the West Bank and Gaza Strip. As Ilana Kass and Bard O'Neill write in *The Deadly Embrace, The Impact of Israeli and Palestinian Rejectionism on the Process*,[2] "the [Palestinian] Islamic groups, Hamas and the IJM [Islamic Jihad], are made up of total rejectionists who unequivocally deny Israel's right to exist because Islamic jurisprudence expressly forbids usurpation of Muslim land and/or the imposition of infidels' authority over Muslims. Both are viewed as cardinal sins the Zionists have committed when they seized Palestinian areas."[3] And: "Hamas and the IJM are . . . reactionary-traditionalists who, as Ziyad Abu-Amr points out, are seeking to transform contemporary societies into communities 'modeled after the first Islamic society.' "[4] Essentially, "the different types of Islamic groups believe in the need to establish an Islamic state, apply Islamic principles, and consider the Koran and the *Sunnah* [sayings and doings of the prophet, established as legally binding precedents] as the basis for all facets of life."[5] Thus "these groups' desired end-state is an Islamic political system in the new Palestine that will ultimately become part of the universal Islamic community (the *umma*)."[6] In Lebanon, "unlike its more moderate Shiite rival [*Amal*] in Lebanon," Hezbollah (the Party of God) "wants Israel. . . expunged from the map of the Middle East . . . . As Sheik Subhi al-Tufayli, *Hezbollah*'s former Secretary General and, subsequently, its representative in the al-Biqa Valley, bluntly put it: "Our goal is to destroy the Zionist entity, and in the near future there won't be a single Jew or Zionist left in Palestine."[7]

Admittedly, the Oslo Accords are defective in two ways: in what they include and what they exclude, and are in need of supplementation, refinement, and other improvements, through further negotiations, preferably before the final settlement stage (not, however, by "redefinition," as Netanyahu apparently wants[8]). Equally important, the peace process must be kept alive, by both parties implementation of its unfulfilled or only partly fulfilled provisions, including the Wye Agreement. Fortunately, Israel's agreement, pursuant to the Wye Agreement, to pull out of an additional 13% of the West Bank, should forestall warnings such as those of Laura Zittrain Eisenberg and Neil Caplan who wrote, echoing Arafat's earlier warnings, that "even more telling than the dangers of unfulfilled expectations, the situation on the ground is also subject to rapid deterioration. Continued short-outs between Israeli soldiers and Palestinian protestors or fugitives and the perpetuation of special privileges for Jewish settlers are sparks ready to rekindle the *Intifada*. If Netanyahu makes good on campaign pledges to expand Israeli settlements and bring thousands more Jews into the West Bank, the tinderbox will likely explode."[9]

According to these authors, part of the reason for the Palestinian and Israeli disappointment with the peace process is that the PLO and Israeli leadership

> failed to communicate to their people a realistic understanding of what has been accomplished. . . . In Israel, the accord was often referred to as a peace agreement, rather than, simply as an agreement that might ultimately culminate in peace. Among Palestinians, there was widespread perception, which the leadership did not try very vigorously to dispel, that this was an agreement on Palestinian independence, rather than simply an agreement on a process that might fulfill that aspiration (Haller 1994, 59).[10]

Full Palestinian autonomy, if and when attained, would be the very first instance of Palestinian self-rule in Palestine's checkered history. That, and its great potential as a stepping-stone to statehood, should make its full, firm political and psychological support the only rational course for the Islamist critics of the Accords and the peace process, Palestinian, and others, to help to strengthen the PNA's hand in its dealings and negotiations with Israel, helping to move the peace process forward toward full autonomy and Palestinian statehood. For, according to Yvonne Yazbeck Haddad,[11] fully 30% of Palestinians in the West Bank and Gaza support Hamas (and Islamic Jihad?), while recent polls showed that 70% of Palestinians residing in the occupied territories supported the peace process.[12]

Perhaps nothing would help the peace process and the Palestinian cause more than for Hamas and Islamic Jihad to give up all suicide bombings and other acts of violence against Israel,[13] which led to the near collapse of the peace process—only revived by the Wye Agreement, thanks largely to President Bill Clinton's efforts. Putting an end to these desperate and bloody acts would also spare innocent Palestinian as well as Israeli lives. Indeed, in addition to being morally abhorrent, the violence that Hamas and other militant Islamists have perpetrated in their attempt to scuttle the peace process is a palpable example of cutting one's nose to spite one's face. The militants' goal of destroying Israel and "liberating" the whole of Palestine is just a fantasy having no relation to reality, even if it were morally and legally justified.

According to Haddad, the Islamists, aware of the present military weakness of Arab and Islamic countries, project their liberation of Palestine a hundred years hence. But how is that magic number supposed to change the military equation, given that Israel's military superiority is bound to continue during the twenty-first century, by virtue of its great technological advantage over the Arabs, and its great superiority in the air and on the ground, thanks in good measure to U.S. military beneficence. Israel's increasing military ties to Turkey is another important factor (see later). Even if, by a stretch of the imagination, some Arab state, say Iraq, were able to increase its military power tenfold in the coming century, despite the U.S.'s and the UN's unremitting efforts to prevent it from regaining its antebellum military capability, it would be foolhardy for it to risk Israel's nuclear response to any missile attack it may contemplate. As in this century, time will almost certainly be on Israel's side in the twenty-first century and beyond.

Above all, what would happen to the very people, the Palestinian masses, allegedly for whose sake the militants are willing to continue their struggle for another century? Can *they,* and their children and grandchildren, endure another century of suffering and misery, until their supposed deliverance? And is it *democratic* or *fair* for a minority to expect the majority to do so without their being asked, and so, without their consent?

In what she labels "Initial Islamist Assessment," "the first written responses outlining objections," Haddad lists sixteen Islamist objections to the Oslo Accords, which she summarizes from an article by Professor Sami Al-Araian of Tampa, Florida. In what follows, I shall evaluate the most important of the objections.

The objections are of two sorts. (A) The majority are essentially criticisms of putative serious deficiencies in the Accords. That is, what the critics consider to be crucial Palestinian concerns the Accords fail to address, together with agreements they believe accede too much to Israel. (B) The remaining objections pertain to what the Islamists believe are the Accords' baleful consequences for the Palestinians. But some of the objections under (A) or (B) impugn Israel's intentions and motives, concerns, and aims, in excluding matters of great concern to Palestinians, or in forcing on them restrictions that exclusively serve Israel's interests.

The first objection I shall consider is that so-called Palestinian self-rule is not genuine self-rule at all: that the Accords keep "*all political, economic and military cards in the hands of the Israelis.*"[14] The Palestinian administrative council's powers are "restricted to six service-type areas, which only exacerbates Palestinian fears that the aim of this agreement is simply to relieve the Israeli army from having to rule the Palestinians 'without giving up the claims over the land, water, and ultimate sovereignty over the territories.'"[15] Haddad comments that Al-Araian worries that, in the end, Palestinian self-rule will be like the "Bantustan townships in South Africa under the apartheid system" (Al-Araian, p. 8).[16] The "redeployment of Israeli forces" that the Accords speak about are not genuine withdrawals from the territories, since, as Al-Araian points out, the territory the Accords promise the Palestinians is "less than 1.5% of the land of Palestine." The anticipated implementation of UN Resolutions 242 and 338, "in which international law would be upheld forcing Israel to give up land it acquired through war," did not occur. Israel continues to hold on to the land it seized (p. 8).[17]

The objection is obviously correct with regard to what the peace process and autonomy had failed to accomplish at the time the article was written, as well as at the time of this writing. But it ignores the fact that the agreements reached in 1993 pertained to the final settlement at the end of the transitional stage. I quote "Article I. AIM OF THE NEGOTIATIONS:

> The aim of the Israeli-Palestinian negotiations within the current Middle East peace process is, among other things, to establish a Palestinian Interim Self-Government Authority, the elected Council . . . , for the Palestinian people in the West Bank and the Gaza Strip, for a transitional period not exceeding five years, leading to a permanent settlement based on Security Council Resolutions 242 and 338.[18]

In fact, an error underlying *all* of Al-Araian's objections is his assumption that the transitional, autonomy stage is the be and end of all, and so, signals the demise of Palestinian hopes for an independent state.

Nevertheless, it is extremely frustrating, particularly for the Palestinians in the West Bank and Gaza Strip, that even now, four whole years after the accords were signed, Israel has only now begun to redeploy its troops, which, if completed in January 1999 in accordance with the Wye Agreement, would have added an additional 13% of the West Bank to the 27% the Palestinians received from the previous, Labor administration. During the past two years, only part (80%) of Hebron was returned to the Palestinians but the present administration, thanks to persistent mediation of Dennis Ross, the U.S. Special Envoy. In the meantime, Israel had not only not stopped the expansion of Jewish settlements in the West Bank but had given the go-ahead to the building of a housing project in East Jerusalem, heedless of U.S. and UN criticism, Palestinian protests, and violent Palestinian-Israeli confrontations.

Of particular importance in the present context was Yasser Arafat's "historic speech to the United Nations General Assembly" on September 28, 1998, in which he appealed,

> for support for a Palestinian state but pointedly did not repeat a controversial vow to declare one unilaterally if Israel did not go along.
> Arafat urged the General Assembly to 'stand by our people,' and stressed that the Oslo peace accords demand of us to shoulder our responsibilities and they await the establishment of their independent state,' he said.
> 'This independent Palestinian state must be established as an embodiment of the right of our people to self-determination.' "Arafat's speech before the General Assembly had particular significance: Never before had Arafat—or any other Palestinian—addressed the audience from the podium during the regular debate. The Palestinian observer mission was granted that right earlier this summer.
> Arafat closed his speech by saying he looked forward to speaking to the General Assembly when Palestine is 'an independent state, when peace has prevailed in the land of peace and in the entire Middle East.'[19]

"*The Palestinian demand to halt the construction of settlements, at least the building of new ones, in the Occupied Territories has been totally ignored*" (p. 9).[20] As stated, this objection is perfectly valid. The construction or expansion of settlements is the legacy of the Begin and Shamir governments' hard-line policy of creating "facts on the ground, with a view to preventing the creation of a Palestinian state, or, at present, to keep as much of the West Bank under Israeli control as possible, in the event of Palestinian statehood.

"*The status of Jerusalem, so important as a holy city to both Muslims and Christians, has basically been ignored in the agreement, with the acknowledgment that its status would be negotiated later.* 'What else,' asks Al-Araian, 'could the Palestinians possibly give the Israelis [now?] for them to give up part of Jerusalem?' (p, 9)."[21]

In retrospect, given the recent two-year stalemate in the peace process, and Palestinian "bitterness [that] was the overriding theme,"[22] it would have been greatly desirable if, among other burning issues, the future of East Jerusalem and of the Palestinian refugees could have been dealt with in the Oslo Accords—were that at all possible. But given the great complexity and sensitivity of the former subject, which we already saw in chapter 3, it would have been practically impossible for the two sides meaningfully to consider, let alone agree on the future status of East Jerusalem during the Oslo Accords. Only in the context, and as part of, the final settlement regarding the West Bank and Gaza Strip as a whole, could that be possible.

With regard to the Palestinian refugee problem, Al-Araian states, in Haddad's words, that "*there is no attempt in the Accords to address the issue of the fate of 4 million Palestinians living as refugees in the diaspora. This goes against UN resolutions acknowledging the right of Palestinians to return to their homeland or to be compensated. Thus, by definition the Accords lack the support of two-thirds of all Palestinians.* 'While Israel prepares to absorb as many as 2 million Russian Jews and U.S. Jewish settlers, it continues to deprive the true owners of the land, the Palestinians, from living there'" (p. 9).[23] But what I said about the future of East Jerusalem applies, *mutatis mutandis*, to this very important human problem.[24] Specifically: since the number of refugees who could be resettled in the West Bank and Gaza Strip depends on the space and resources available in the future Palestinian state, that question cannot be profitably dealt with until the two sides agree about the precise extent of the territory that would fall under Palestinian sovereignty.

But no compelling reasons would serve to justify the nonimplementation of Article V of the Declaration Of Principles, "TRANSITIONAL PERIOD AND PERMANENT STATUS NEGOTIATIONS," when September 2000 comes round; for then, as Article 3 states, "[permanent status].... negotiations shall cover remaining issues, including: Jerusalem, refugees, settlements, security arrangements, borders, relations and cooperation with other neighbors, and other issues of common interest."[25] Surely the secret negotiations about the creation of a fake "Jerusalem" as the putative future capital of a Palestinian state, described in chapter 3, cannot count as genuine negotiations about the "real" Jerusalem! The latest episode in the ongoing Jerusalem saga is that, on June 21, 1998, the Israeli cabinet approved a plan to "expand the City of Jerusalem beyond its current borders, despite angry protests from Palestinians and Washington's warning that the plan was 'provocative.'"[26] Netanyahu defended it in a news conference after the unanimous decision, saying, among other things, that "the plan had no political ramifications and was not a violation of the Israeli-Palestinian peace accords, under which the final status of Jerusalem is to be negotiated with the Palestinians." The newspaper adds that the plan is "for strengthening of Jerusalem's status, . . . in part by annexing several Israeli towns in the 'Jerusalem corridor' to the west, and in part by bringing several Jewish communities and settlements on lands conquered in 1967 to the east and north under an 'umbrella municipality,' with Jerusalem responsible for planning, construction, budget matters and services."[27] Netanyahu also said that "all this, . . . within Israel's right, and 'an internal Israeli matter, not a matter requiring a diplomatic report'":[28] clearly implying, of course, the constant Israeli position that Jerusalem as a whole is an integral part of Israel.[29]

As far as the Jewish settlements referred to by Al-Araian above, it is imperative that the Israeli government stop all settlement construction or expansion. Unfortunately, that has yet to occur. *"The PLO negotiating team has failed to deal specifically with the more than 13,000 Palestinians who are imprisoned or detained in Israeli jails"* (p. 9).[30] This is a serious human problem, particularly given the extremely harsh conditions that prevail in Israeli jails,[31] and the Israelis' employment of a certain form of torture to extract information from suspected terrorists.[32] Since the publication of Al-Araian's article, Israel has periodically released small numbers of Palestinian prisoners; but since the suicide bombings in 1997, prisons in Israel, and the West Bank and Gaza, have swelled with new political prisoners. On September 4, 1997, after another suicide bombing in West Jerusalem, the PNA arrested a number of militant Hamas leaders under Israeli pressure. The same implication that it is an internal matter underlay Israel's unilateral opening of a second entrance to the tunnel next to the Al-Aqsa mosque. After the Wye Agreement, Israel released 250 Palestinian prisoners, 150 of whom are common criminals, but refused to release any political prisoners, which was viewed by Palestinians as a violation of the agreement, and resulted in violent protests. That, together with the stabbing death of a Palestinian by a suspected Israeli, and the beating almost to death of an Israeli soldier by Palestinian students, brought Israeli withdrawal to a screeching halt. "The Palestinians had expected Israel to release so-called security prisoners—those who fought the Israeli occupation of the West Bank and Gaza Strip" in the 1967 Six Day War. But Netanyahu has no intention to "release murderers or to release Hamas members."[33]

In retrospect, in view of the constant friction and conflict between Palestinians and Israel concerning Palestinian prisoners, perhaps the Accords should have dealt specifically with the status of Palestinian political prisoners in Israeli jails, and under what conditions they would be released; in addition to guarantees that Israel would respect the human and civil rights of Palestinian political prisoners, including suspected or convicted terrorists. For instance, suspects would be expeditiously charged and tried in a fair public trial, and no coercion or torture in any form would be used to extract information or confessions from them.

"*It [the accord] also has failed to deal with the status of the million Palestinians living in occupied lands since 1948 who would remain under the control of Israel,*" "undesirables in their own lands simply because they are not Jews" (p. 10).[34] This objection assumes that the entire former Palestine rightfully belongs to the Palestinians, and ignores the rights of the Jews to a part of the land.

"*In Al-Araian's view, the Accords represent a grave security risk for all Palestinians, because they are not granted constitutional, political, or human rights. Arafat's job of taming the Palestinian resistance and stopping the intifada serves to safeguard Israeli (especially settler) interests at the expense of the Palestinians. Palestinian communities are thus at the mercy of the army and the armed settlers anywhere, including Gaza and Jericho*" (p. 10).[35] Unfortunately, this situation has continued. Frequent clashes between Palestinians and Jewish settlers have occurred, for example in Hebron, where a tiny group of armed Jewish settlers, guarded by the Israeli military, lives cheek by jowl with the unarmed Palestinian majority. Bloody clashes between Palestinian police and Israeli soldiers have also occurred in Gaza and the Old City of Jerusalem.

Al-Araian also objects that *"while political matters were left vague, economic issues were spelled out expansively,"* with Israel's aim to dominate and control "Palestinian economic development, the continuation of Palestinian cheap labor, the expansion of Palestinian consumers, and the inclusion of a much larger market in the Arab world through a small segment of Palestinians acting as agents and middlemen for Israeli products" (p. 10).[36]

Political matters were bound to be left vague, since as we saw, the Accords concentrated on the transitional autonomy stage, leaving other crucial matters to later negotiations. But Al-Araian is partly correct about the economic exploitation of Palestinians: partly correct because, without the (cheap) labor of Palestinian workers in Israel, unemployment in the West Bank and Gaza Strip would be considerably greater; witness the worsening of the Palestinians' economic condition with every border closing. It is to be hoped that if and when a Palestinian state is created, the great economic disadvantage that drives Palestinians to work in Israel as cheap labor will gradually diminish, with economic and technical aid from the United Nations, the United States, and Europe. If these things transpire, Palestinians who desire to work in Israel should be able to demand equal pay for equal work as their Israeli counterparts. So far, much of the international economic aid that Arafat was after from the Accords has not materialized, and many Palestinians are now in direr straits than before autonomy. If the more than $3 billion pledged by the U.S. and 42 other nations on November 30, 1998, at a one-day conference at the State Department in Washington, D.C. materialize during the coming five years, creating the projected half-million jobs on the West Bank and Gaza, it should greatly alleviate Palestinian poverty. And as President Clinton stated at the conference, "No peace stands a chance of lasting if it does not deliver real results to ordinary people."[37] A substantially strengthened economy should reduce the Palestinians' sense of the peace process's failure to improve their lives.

"The treaty [sic] is based on integration of the Zionist regime into the region, a new Middle East order with Israel at the center, sharing the water resources and raw materials of the Arab countries (p. 10). 'Acceptance of this agreement simply guarantees the strategic imbalance of power in favor of Israel and preserves its hegemony and strategic control ([Al-Araian], p. 11).'"[38]

Israel's integration into the region, without any Middle Eastern country necessarily being economically or militarily at its center, is not something objectionable but, on the contrary, much to be desired. Whether Israel in fact becomes the economic center of the region would very much depend on whether the Arab states respond *positively* and *creatively* to Israel's powerful economic challenge by developing their own natural, economic, and human resources—not least their woman power—and collaborating as well as competing with Israel (see chapter 6). The military imbalance is bound to continue, at least as long as Israel feels threatened by Syria, Iraq, or Iran. If peace between Syria and Israel follows Palestinian independence (hence between Lebanon and Israel), and *if* Iran gives its blessing to the limited Palestinian state, the arms race in the region should substantially diminish.

Still, one cannot be very optimistic that this would happen anytime soon, given Israel's continuing military buildup and modernization, e.g., with American help, and its close ties with Turkey, a traditional enemy of the Arabs (or vice versa).[39] On the Iraqi side, the UN arms inspectors reported to the United States in 1996 and 1997 that "they had credible intelligence indicating that Iraq built and has maintained three or four 'implosion devices' that lack only cores of enriched uranium to make 20-kiloton nuclear weapons, according to U.S. government and UN sources."[40] Unfortunately, the UN inspections for hidden Iraqi weapons of mass destruction has come to an end, perhaps permanently.

"It also weakens the position of many non-Zionist Jews [few but vocal, Al-Araian says] *who have supported Palestinian rights"* (p. 11).[41]

What Al-Araian has in mind is unclear. The objection cannot refer to the near fifty-percent of Israeli Jews who supported the Accords and the peace process, and those, including some Zionists, who supported Rabin's and Perez' "land for peace," whose numbers have since increased. Nor, given the Islamists' position, could it refer to the few non-Zionist Jews (such as Noam Chomsky and others Jewish intellectuals/authors referred to in chapter 3) who have proposed the creation of a secular Arab-Jewish state, contrary to what Al-Araian has in mind in speaking of the "God-given rights" of the future generations of Palestinians" (p. 12).[42]

Al-Araian faults Arafat for the secret negotiations that concluded in Oslo. He claims that they "*do not earn the trust and support of the people. They represent an agreement forced on the weaker party, which is then coerced into making painful, unacceptable, and illegal concessions.*"[43]

The objection commits a non sequitur and a factual error. (Compare the U.S.- North Vietnam negotiations that brought the Vietnam War to an end.) Given the patent fact that the Palestinians were the weaker party, it is unrealistic to think that Arafat and his advisers could have gotten most, let alone all, of what they wanted.⁴⁴ Compromise on the Palestinian no less than the Israeli side was essential for any agreement to be reached. Again, the objection that "No single person (i.e., Arafat) should have the right to make such a major decision on behalf of a people. No individual has the right to deprive future generations of their God-given rights,"⁴⁵ ignores the fact that the Palestinians as well as the Arab countries had confirmed the PLO as the sole representative of the Palestinian people, with Yasser Arafat at its head. It would undoubtedly have been more democratic, had that been possible, for Arafat to have had a referendum on the articles of the Israel-PLO Oslo Declaration of Principles. Even then it is unlikely that the majority of West Bank and Gaza Strip Palestinians would have rejected it, since no widespread Palestinian protests occurred when the Declarations were made public.⁴⁶ True, the majority of Palestinians live in the Diaspora; consequently, a valid referendum would have had to include them. What the outcome of such a worldwide referendum would have been is anyone's guess.

Haddad summarizes Al-Araian's objections succinctly as follows:

> the Islamic critique notes that the Peace Accords took care of several of Israel's concerns. It gave Israel the responsibility for Israelis in the Occupied Territories, kept Jerusalem out of the area of self-government, recognized the right of Israel to exist in secure borders, ended armed resistance, abrogated thirty-three articles from the Palestine National Covenant that called for the eradication of Israel, and altered the core principles of the Palestine Liberation Organization.⁴⁷

The Islamists were not alone in being disappointed by the Oslo Accords. For example, Edward Said, for instance, wrote: "Let us call the [Oslo] agreement by its real name: an instrument of Palestinian surrender, a Palestinian Versailles."⁴⁸ Hanan Ashrawi, who played an important role in the negotiations that led to the Oslo Accords and the peace process, describes her disappointment in her 1994 book, as follows:

> As 1993 melted into 1994, Palestinian-Israeli negotiations entered into a sliding time frame and the talks seemed to diminish in scope and substance. Gradually, Israeli priorities, diction, and approaches began to surface, and to take priority over our conceptual and semantic plan. Substance was ceded for technicalities and procedures, fragmentation replaced the integrated comprehensive perspective; the asymmetry of power was fully incorporated into the process. Israel not only persisted in creating unilateral facts to prejudge the outcome, particularly of postponed issues such as Jerusalem and the settlements, it also placed the PLO on probation, in a never-ending test of good behavior. Many Palestinians, including prominent intellectuals and political leaders, started speaking out in public against the slippery slope of peacemaking under coercion and duress.⁴⁹

In sum, the following are the most crucial defects of the Oslo Accords as I see them: (a) At a minimum, the Declaration of Principles ought to have stated that it "looked with favor" upon eventual Palestinian sovereignty in the West Bank and Gaza Strip, and that the final settlement stage would include negotiations regarding Palestinian sovereignty: (b) The five-year maximum transitional period is too long. A period of, say, three years would have spared both parties a lot of unnecessary conflict and bloodshed; (c) Pursuant to (b), Israel ought to have agreed to the speedy withdrawal from the greater part of the occupied territories.

The Islamist objections to the Oslo Accords and the peace process involved a deeper ideological difference between them and those non-Islamist Palestinians who were also critical of the peace process, on the one hand, and the pro-PLO Palestinians who accepted it, with or without reservations. That meant in practice that Hamas and Islamic Jihad would continue to target Israeli civilians and military with a series of bloody suicide bombings,[50] albeit wisely refrained from attacking Palestinian political figures, or Israeli Jews living in Gaza. As Jean-François Legrain observes, "This attitude [of not attacking Palestinian political figures or Israelis residing in Gaza] reflects an extreme realism *vis-à-vis* the autonomy. HAMAS accepted the Oslo agreement as a fact and is now forging the movement's new politics. Such pragmatism[51] lends strength to the desire of some HAMAS leaders to transform the movement into an opposition party."[52] And Raji Sourani, director of the Palestinian Center for Human Rights, proclaimed: "Free, [Sheik] Yassin stands to build Hamas's credibility as a political force. Yassir Arafat already has been hurt by his inability to push forward the peace process, and his Palestinian Authority government is widely perceived as corrupt. 'He [Yassin] is going to unify Hamas.'"[53] But that transformation has yet to occur. Soon after his release, Yassin "offered Netanyahu a ceasefire in return for a total Israeli withdrawal from the territories and the release of all Palestinian prisoners—evidently without consulting Arafat."[54] Further, "some observers read moderation in Yassin's initial comments" after leaving jail, since his proposal "seemed to acknowledge at least Israel's pre-1967 borders," "rather than (as the Islamists in general do) promising to "liberate our land and establish a Muslim Palestinian state."[55]

Legrain notes that "the return to religion, more than the recently adopted armed struggle, appears in HAMAS's literature as the preferred expression of jihad, as suggested by the slogan "Islam is the solution and the option."[56] "The normative discourse on the basic illegitimacy of Israel's existence and its inevitable destruction can be converted into various—

even contradictory—daily practices, including a more or less temporary coexistence with the Israeli state."[57]

With that, we turn to Israeli rejectionism.

III

Israeli Rejectionism

In the Preface to their *The Deadly Embrace*,[58] a work devoted to a detailed "comparative analysis of (radical) Israeli and Palestinian rejectionism,"[59] Ilana Kass and Bard O'Neill note that they "found that . . . [the] fundamentalist mutation [of the Palestinian resistance] has a mirror image on the Israeli side, where equally committed believers espouse remarkably similar—if mutually exclusive—agendas. These rejectionists are united in their near-term objective of destroying peace, but ultimately sworn to destroy each other."[60] The authors correctly argue that "the threat posed by [radical] Israeli rejectionism, if left unchecked, is potentially greater [than the threat of Palestinian rejectionism], since it imperils not only peace, but also [Israel's] democracy and the rule of law."[61] And Israeli rejectionists are an "increasingly active insurgency, complete with a unique world view and a fully-fledged action program," and are a "well-organized, dedicated and militant political group, with a significant lease of popular support."[62]

Some Israeli rejectionists are religious, others secular; and some are pragmatic; but their common strategic position is the refusal to trade land for peace. Their "overarching commitment [is] to keep the Land of Israel, in its post-1967 boundaries, under undivided Jewish control."[63] They believe that the end justifies the means, and so, "to facilitate the attainment of . . . [their] goal, they have been ready to maneuver in many directions, employing a variety of tactics: legal, quasi-legal and illegal."[64]

The radical right is uncompromising in its dislike even for the present very limited Palestinian territorial autonomy and would like nothing better than to roll it back, which is reflected in some episodes intended to foment religious conflict (possibly, even war) between Palestinians (indeed, Muslims in general) and Israelis.

At the heart of the ideological and political divisions between these extreme right or total rejectionists and the more moderate Israelis (corresponding to the ideological and political divisions between the Islamists and non-Islamists[65]) is religion, which has torn the whole country apart. In a May 1998 article in *Time* magazine, the Israeli author A.B. Yehoshua was quoted as saying that "as Israel celebrates its 50th anniversary, its citizens identify the rift over religion as their No.1 problem. With the country well established and peace in the region a growing reality, Israelis are fighting among themselves as never before."66 "For 50 years, we had an external enemy who obliged us to lower the tenor of our internal tensions."67 "But the external enemy doesn't unite us anymore."68 Similarly, Menachem Friedman, a sociologist at Bar-Ilan University in Ramat Gan, stated: "The ensuing struggle is nasty and getting nastier. . . . We are really near the edge [of] where people can tolerate each other."69 And,

> The conflict is rooted in an old and unresolved question of national identity: Is Israel a Jewish state, with the emphasis on Jewish, or is it a state for the Jews, a regular, modern, democratic place where Jews are in the majority? Israel's Zionist founders were almost exclusively secular—in many respects, antireligious—and they saw Judaism principally as a nationality. But in deference to tradition, and as a way of securing the support of the Orthodox minority, they made certain concessions to religion. . . . In the past 20 years, religious political parties extracted further allowances as they joined various governmental coalitions.70

> Relations [in Israel] with the Palestinians are another fault line [in addition to the religious rift among the Jews in Israel]. Some 56% of secular Israelis support the peace process, compared with only 9% of the *haredim* and 24% of the so-called modern Orthodox. One group of rabbis went so far as to instruct army soldiers to disobey any order to withdraw from parts of the West Bank, an invitation to insurrection. A survey last fall showed that 27% of religious teenagers condone the murder of Rabin.71

Marginalization of Islamist and Israeli Rejectionists

Kass and O'Neill note that the attempt to marginalize the Islamist and Israeli rejectionists involves the "fundamental choice between a policy of inclusion or exclusion," although, as they say, implementing these options "would require difficult choices among competing courses of action and, at times, among equally distasteful alternatives."72

Marginalization of Islamist Rejectionists

Kass and O"Neill believe that "more than anything, the peace process has turned the tables: While land remains the center of gravity, now it is Israel to be called upon to cede increasingly significant portions of the territory it controls. Thus, a new asymmetry is emerging, wherein, for the first time this century, the Palestinians are on the winning side of the territorial equation. Correspondingly, as the Palestinians' key exoteric grievances are gradually being satisfied, loss of land is fast becoming the primary factor driving Israeli rejectionism."73 "This led to tacit cooperation in attaining such shared short-term objectives as toppling the Labor government—an aim explicitly espoused by both Islamic militants and the entire Israeli right."[74]

But the little that has been accomplished can hardly be described as the Palestinians' being "on the winning side of the territorial equation." Similarly with the satisfaction of their "key exoteric grievances." For example, no sooner than Israel began withdrawing from parts of the West Bank stipulated by the Wye Agreement began, than violent Palestinian protests broke out over Palestinian political prisoners still held in Israeli jails. So far, only 27% of the West Bank and Gaza Strip has been ceded by Israel in what can only be described as a very modest or weak form of autonomy.

It is true that the small groups of partial rejectionists, such as the PFLP and the DFLP, should be "further marginalized by encouraging their open participation in the electoral process." Since Marxism presently has little appeal in the Arab world, their marginalization should not pose any significant risks, as our authors point out.[75] Thus their participation in "mainstream politics" would not threaten the majority non-Marxist governing PNA in future elections.

Our authors likewise believe that groups like the Islamic National Salvation Party, "which consistently eschew violence and adhere to democratic procedures," should be allowed to participate in the political process. In their view, "the risk that such inclusion would redound to the rejectionists' favor is outweighed by the gains that could accrue from tempering and splitting the movement."[76] This is sound advice, provided these parties are willing to participate in the Palestinian political process, and are encouraged (or even allowed) by the PNA to do so.

The serious political and military threats to the PNA, to the Palestinian autonomy in general, and to the peace process, both internally and *vis-a-vis* Israel, arise not from the preceding groups but from Hamas and Palestinian Islamic Jihad. Since, as we saw, these groups reject the Accords and the peace process, our authors propose their "exclusion from participation in the autonomous government"—by, I, assume, banning their military wing from the political process, but allowing, indeed encouraging, their social wing to continue their beneficent social and educational work. But banning them—worse, trying to crush them—would be contrary to the very democracy that needs to be fostered, not hindered, in the autonomous region; particularly, as noted earlier, these groups have not used violence against the PNA. Attempts to ban or crush them are also fraught with danger for the autonomous region's fragile peace and stability, and for the peace process as a whole. They would also be doomed to fail. They would encourage, not stop, further strikes against Israel. Nothing any government or people can do—especially within the bounds of morality and the law—can completely prevent determined terrorists from committing acts of violence. I therefore believe that it is even more important than in the case of the other Palestinian groups, for the PNA to try to include Hamas and Islamic Jihad in the political process: not by inviting them to join the PNA but by allowing, even encouraging them to form an opposition political party, as some members of Hamas expressed interest in doing. No such political party has so far been formed.

The reality, of course, is that Arafat has been under Israeli pressure to "counter" terrorism; for example, by disrupting the terrorist cells. But any serious attempt to do so (assuming that Arafat's police could find out their location) and disarm Hamas and Islamic Jihad, would have almost certainly led to violent confrontations between them and Palestinian security forces, and may well have destabilized the entire autonomous region.

If the present autonomy is to lead to Palestinian sovereignty, realism or pragmatism, if nothing else, demands that the militants (a) commit no new acts of violence against Israel, and (b) Israel and the PNA quickly move to the full implementation of the Wye Agreement, as well as all other outstanding articles of the Accords' transitional stage; (c) Israel and the PNA should then proceed to the creation of a Palestinian state in the autonomous region. Among the important issues that would be negotiated would be the drawing of permanent boundaries between Israel and the new state.

Palestinian independence should partially (even if only temporarily) satisfy the Islamists, transforming them into partial rejectionists, eager to join the Palestinian political process if for no other reason than to further their own ultimate political goals. With statehood a reality, realism should prevent them from attempting to seize power to establish a fundamentalist Islamic state; cognizant of the fact that any attempts of that kind would bring swift Israeli military intervention and an end to Palestinian statehood. True, the return to religion—as suggested by the slogan, "Islam is the solution and the option"[77]—is the Islamists' final goal, and armed struggle, its necessary means. Still, with "sulh" in place as a result of Israel's having "veered toward peace" by granting Palestinian independence, militant Islamists should be willing to put off the armed struggle for decades, if not for "one hundred years."

Marginalization of Israeli Rejectionism
Despite the risks involved, which they correctly note are "significant," Kass and O'Neill essentially recommend the marginalization of the total, far-right Israeli rejectionists, religious and secular, by their possible inclusion,

under certain conditions, "in the governing coalition"; because of their belief that there are "clear merits in broadening the basis of support for the incumbent government's policies."[78] But for reasons, some of which they mention, I believe the risks would be significantly greater than the benefits they envisage.

The first risk is that "flexibility is often the price of consensus."[79] That is, there is a likelihood of the government's "being hamstrung by a series of crisscrossing agreements and back-room deals. The inevitable result would be policy paralysis and further erosion of the peace process."[80] The right's heterogeneity "would only exacerbate mutual animosities and deepen the secular-religious divide, particularly if the true believers were to hinge their support"— as they would naturally do—"on promotion of their parochial domestic agendas."[81] Indeed, considering the plethora of Israeli political parties, each with its different agenda, and the realities of the political situation in Israel during 50 years of its modern history, the inclusion of even a few of these parties in the governing coalition would almost certainly spell chaos and paralysis.

Soon after he took office in July 1999, Prime Minister Ehud Barak met with Yasser Arafat, President Clinton, and Husni Mubarak of Egypt. In early statements he indicated that, in addition to implementing the Wye Agreement, he hoped to "proceed toward a final agreement with the Palestinians." But aides say that the "Syrians are his first priority. With the Palestinians, Barak can expect drawn-out negotiations involving issues like the status of Jerusalem and the future of the Jewish settlements in the Palestinian territories. By contrast, a Syrian deal could come quickly—possibly within a year."[82] As far as the Wye Agreement is concerned, Barak would "prefer not to carry out Wye at all but instead proceed directly to negotiations on a final peace treaty with the Palestinians."[83] Less than a month after, his proposal to "dovetail the Wye implementation into final status talks"—with the second Israeli withdrawal to take place after October 1, 1999[84]—led to his and Arafat's first public squabble, as Arafat's cabinet quickly rejected the proposal, demanding that Barak should start the [second] withdrawal "within three weeks."[85]

A second problem our authors point out, which continually faced Netanyahu's Likud party since it came to power, and which would have come back to haunt it had it been returned to power, was that its "ability and will to temper the radical rejectionists' proclivity to violence remains to be treated." [86]

Given these difficulties, our authors propose that,

> any cooperation with the radical right must include an iron-clad commitment to shun violence. . . . The assassination of Prime Minister Rabin—universally con-

demned across the Israeli political spectrum—could be used as an object-lesson to dramatize the tragic consequences of political violence, thus compelling as many rejectionists as possible to publicly recommit themselves to the rule of law. For those who value their solemn word, such a vow might suffice. Otherwise, nothing short of literal excommunication, followed by a persistent, determined educational effort and leadership by example would be required.[87]

Some of the suggestions in the preceding passage are naive and impractical, but others are worth pursuing. It is almost certain that many or all of the total rejectionists, particularly the armed Jewish settlers, e.g., in Gaza and Hebron, where they are vastly outnumbered by the unarmed Palestinian population, would simply refuse to make such an iron-clad commitment.. Again, what our authors mean by the "literal excommunication" of those who "refuse to publicly recommit themselves to the rule of law," it must be assumed, is the rejectionists' exclusion from the political process, not banning their parties, which would violate the very democracy that, rightly for our authors, is the raison d'etre of the far right's being "compelled to shun violence." For as they say, "democracy is based on willingness to abide by the rules of the game."[88] Consequently, the only justifiable, albeit uncertain, way to marginalize them—not exclude them from the political process—would be through the use of educational methods similar to, or adapted from, those used by The Interfaith Alliance in the United States, which is "working to make sure that religious political extremists [the Christian Right] do not have the only voice regarding the direction of our nation."[89] The Alliance is doing so by

> Shining The Light On Extremism. . . . They conduct voter guides—to ensure that voters know the real agenda of candidates running for. . . . office. Public Education and Voter Mobilization. . . . public forums to educate their communities on the agenda and tactics of religious political extremists. Alliances are holding educational events to ensure their voices are heard in public policy debates, and they are mobilizing *all* Americans to vote.
>
> Monitoring and Responding. . . . alliances are monitoring the country's governing bodies . . . to ensure that the extreme right does not use religion as a weapon to impose their political agendas on our communities or our nation.
>
> Providing a National Voice: TIA's national board of Directors consists of mainstream religious leaders who provide a strong, interfaith voice on a national level. They have reached millions of Americans through television, newspaper and radio interviews. They work to ensure that an alternative faith-based voice is heard in the ongoing dialogue regarding the future of our nation." [90]

In "The real fight in Israel pits secular against Orthodox," Thomas Friedman describes Israeli efforts to overcome what he calls the "cultural war" in Israel, especially adapted to the task since it springs from the actual conditions that prevail in the country. First, the juridical response to the cultural war is led by the Supreme Court chief justice, Aharon Barak, who is trying to use the court to create a "constitutional framework" which will "preserve individual rights and keep the centrifugal forces ... in check." Second, to "reject ... the ultra-Orthodox interpretation of Judaism" dominating Israel, and to try to develop an "alternative that can bridge religious and secular and embrace modernity." Third, the political response is to bring together the "moderate religious Jews of the Likud ... [and] the moderate secularists of Labor to forge a new nationalism," not dependent on the ultra-Orthodox or Labor's Israeli Arabs.[91]

In tandem with the methods Friedman describes, sustained educational efforts are needed to impress upon or to remind the Israeli majority that keeping the Palestinians in an indefinite state of dependency, in their very homeland, strikes at the very heart of the genuine democracy to which they aspire. For as Kass and O'Neill aptly observe,

> Israel's inability to fully solve the Palestinian problem poses a long-term challenge to its democratic nature— as well as to its security. Having effectively drawn a Green Line of democracy, while permitting, since 1967, the routinization of extra-legal behavior beyond it, Israel now faces the risks inherent in fragmenting an essentially indivisible concept. Insofar as there is no such thing as selective or situational democracy, the inevitable outcome has been a progressive erosion of the very values that anchor the nation's existence and assure it of continued Western support.[92]

In an address at Duke University in October 1997, Shimon Perez gave two other compelling reasons—one concerning its security, the other concerning its Jewish character—why Israel ought to grant independence to the Palestinians. He stressed the impossibility of retaining "territory in which there are large Palestinian communities. 'We cannot have 100 percent security unless we give the Palestinians 100 percent freedom. ... [And] if Israel was to try to keep all its land and all its people, it would stop being a Jewish state and it would become bi-national. One state would mean permanent conflict.'" And "'we [Israelis] are able to negotiate out of strength, but we can't forget to negotiate. When you are strong, you can impose war, but you cannot impose peace.'"[93]

To sum up. The defense of Palestinian statehood in the West Bank and Gaza Strip, begun in chapter 3, was continued in this chapter, by an attempt to respond to the Islamists and the radical Israeli right, who agree in their uncompromising rejection of the Oslo Accords and the peace process, including Palestinian autonomy. The former's ultimate aim is the "liberation" of Palestine by the destruction of Israel, and the establishment of an Islamic state based on Islamic Law. The Israeli rejectionists or radical Jewish right dream of a Greater Israel comprising the entire territory of former Palestine, which they consider to be the Biblical Land of Israel promised by God to the Jews.

The response to Palestinian and other Arab-Muslim Islamist rejectionists mainly took the form of an almost point by point reply to Professor Sami Al-Araian's detailed criticism of the Oslo Accords and the peace process. Although Al-Araian's strictures were largely rejected, it was agreed that the Accords left much to be desired about Palestinian territorial rights, because of their failure to deal forthwith with the most crucial issues dividing the Palestinians and Israel, including Palestinian statehood and the future status of Jerusalem, and the fate of the Palestinian refugees. It was also agreed that the Palestinian autonomy resulting from the Oslo Accords gave the Palestinian National Authority too little real power, over too little territory.

Having already attempted to establish the territorial rights of Palestinians to part of the territory in chapter 2, a brief discussion of, and response to, Israeli rejectionism followed. The last section considered some ways of marginalizing Islamic and Israeli rejectionists proposed by Kass and O'Neill in their book *The Deadly Embrace*, and by Thomas Friedman and others in relation to the radical Israeli religious right, and drew a parallel with the methods used by The Interfaith Alliance in the United States, which, as its brochure states, is "working to make sure that religious political extremists [the Christian Right] do not have the only voice regarding the direction of our nation." The chapter concluded with references to Shimon Perez' October 1997 talk at Duke University, in which he gave two important reasons why Palestinian independence was essential for Israel as well as for the Palestinians.

Notes

1. Chief among the abuses have been Arafat's authoritarian management of his office, the absence of free speech, and the use of torture (in some instances, resulting in death) of incarcerated suspects or convicted terrorists.

2. Lanham, New York & London, 1997.

3. Ibid., 226.

4. Ziyad Abu-Amr, *The Islamic Movement in the West Bank and Gaza Strip*, 2. Kass and O'Neill, 226.

5. Ziyad Abu-Amr, "Hamas: A Historical and Political Background," *Journal of Palestine Studies*, Summer 1993, 2. Kass and O'Neill, 226.

6. Op cit., 226. Cf. Benjamin Netanyahu's fear of an Iran-style independent Palestine (see later).

7. Ibid., 228.

8. See later.

9. "The Israeli-Palestinian Peace Process in Historical Perspective," *The Middle East Peace Process, Interdisciplinary Perspectives*, Ilan Peleg, ed. (Albany, NY, 1998), 3–19.

10. Ibid., 17–18.

11. Islamists and the Peace Process," *Political Islam, Revolution, Radicalism, or Reform?* John L. Esposito, ed. (Boulder and London, 1997), 207–229.

12. An article titled "Return of the Sheik," in the October 20, 1997, issue of *Newsweek*, stated that although Hamas officials "claim a following of between 30 and 40 percent of Palestinians, recent polls have put the support at more like 10 to 15 percent (p. 39)." The article predicted that the figures will go up because of the ongoing stalemate between Netanyahu and Arafat, and the power struggle between Hamas and Arafat as a result of Sheik Yassin's return to Gaza. But, in fact, Hamas has avoided such a struggle after Yassin's return.

13. Although they would certainly consider them freedom fighters, not terrorists.

14. Haddad, 208.

15. Ibid., 208–209. My italics.

16. Ibid., 209. In fact, before the Netanyahu government lost power, Israel was reported to be trying to cantonize the West Bank with the Jewish settlements, among other things, in the belief that that would better serve its security. That, together with Israel's plan to fortify the existing Jewish settlements, looked very

much like advance preparations for a possible eventuality: viz., Palestinian statehood.

17 Ibid., 209.

18 Israel-PLO Declaration of Principles (September 13, 1993)," *Arab-Israeli Conflict and Conciliation, A Documentary History*, Bernard Reich, ed. (Westport, Conn. & London, 1995), 231.

19 Ibid.

20 Haddad, op cit. My italics.

21 Ibid. My italics.

22 Ibid.

23 Ibid. My italics.

24 See my suggestions concerning the refugee problem in chapter 3.

25 Bernard Reich, op cit., 232.

26 "Israel plans to expand Jerusalem," *Milwaukee Journal-Sentinel*, June 22, 1998.

27 Ibid.

28 Ibid.

29 The same implication that it is an internal matter underlay Israel's unilateral opening of a second entrance to the tunnel next to the Al-Aqsa mosque in the Old City of Jerusalem.

30 Ibid. My italics.

31 Among the prisoners in Al-Arish jail in the Negev, the harshest in Israel, are those (Palestinians) convicted of terrorism. In a recent program on cable TV, with Bill Curtis, it was stated that the jail's aim is to rehabilitate the prisoners. That, however, I assume, did not apply to the terrorists! For the torture of Palestinian inmates, see, for example, Judith Miller, op cit. See also my *The Morality of Terrorism* (New York, 1998), chapter 6.

32 See, for example, Judith Miller, *God has Ninety-Nine Names* (New York, 1996), and my *The Morality of Terrorism*, chapter 6, "Responses to Terrorism."

33 "Mideast talks break up over prisoner issue," *Milwaukee Journal-Sentinel*, November 30, 1998.

34 Haddad, 209. My italics. Although this seems to exaggerate the treatment of Arab Israelis, there is evidence that, both as individuals and as a group, Israeli Arabs suffer from discrimination. On the other hand, the Knesset includes a number of Arab Israeli deputies

35 Ibid. My italics.

36 Ibid., 209–210. My italics.

37 "Over $3 billion pledged to help Palestinians," *Milwaukee Journal-Sentinel*, November 30, 1998.

38 Haddad, op cit., 210. My italics.

39 See, for example, Marios Evriviades, "Dangerous Liaisons, Turkish-Israeli Axis," *The Armenian Mirror-Spectator*, September 5, 1998; reprinted from the July/August 1998 edition of *Odyssey*.

40 *Milwaukee Journal-Sentinel*, October 3, 1998.

41 Haddad, op cit., 210. My italics.

42 Ibid.

43 Ibid. Cf. Edward Said (not an Islamist): "Let us call the agreement by its real name: an instrument of Palestinian surrender, a Palestinian Versailles." ("The Morning After," *Inquiry*, Spring 1994, 20. Haddad quotes another writer, Uri Davis, "The Declaration of Principles Evokes a Palestinian Nightmare: Not Once Is the Word Sovereignty Mentioned," op cit., 34.)

44 Hanan Ashrawi's *This Side of Peace* (New York, 1995) provides a detailed account of the complexities of the agonized Palestinian negotiations that culminated in the Oslo Agreement, and the Declaration of Principles. See, e.g., 264ff., and later in this chapter.

45 Haddad, op cit., 210.

46 But it is likely that part of the reason for the absence of widespread Palestinian protests was that they were given a rosier picture of what had been agreed on.

47 Salim Ahmad al-Sharif, "al-Sharq al-Awsat al-Jadid," al-Insan 3:12 (October 1944): 7. Haddad, op cit., 210.

48 Quoted by Haddad, op cit., 210, from Al-Araian's article.

49 Op cit., 282.

50 Concerning the ethics of such acts of violence, including suicide bombings, see my *The Morality of Terrorism*, chapters 2 and 4.

51 Judith Miller paints a different picture. She maintains that after the Oslo Accords, Hamas was almost at war with the PLO. See *God Has Ninety Nine Names*, 396f.

52 Jean-Francois Legrain, "HAMAS: Legitimate Heir of Palestinian Nationalism?" *Political Islam*, 173.

53 "Return of the Sheik," *Newsweek*, October 20, 1997, 39.

54 Ibid.

55 Ibid.

56 Legrain, op cit., 175.
57 Ibid.
58 Lanham, New York and London, 1997.
59 Preface, viii.
60 Ibid.
61 Introduction, xvii.
62 Ibid., 75.
63 Ibid.
64 Ibid., 89-90.
65 Cf. "The foundation of the deadly embrace is the assumption—on each side—that the land, in its entirety, belongs exclusively to it." (Kass and O'Neill, op cit., 315.)
66 "The Religious Wars," *Time*, May 11, 1998, 32-34.
67 Ibid., 32.
68 Ibid.
69 Ibid. Also see Thomas L. Friedman, "The Real fight in Israel pits secular against Orthodox," *Milwaukee Journal-Sentinel*, July 1, 1998. Reprinted from the *New York Times*.
70 *Time*, op cit., 32.
71 Ibid., 34. Italics in original.
72 *The Deadly Embrace*, 323-324.
73 Ibid., 313.
74 Ibid., 315.
75 Ibid., 324.
76 Ibid.
77 Legrain, op cit., 175.
78 Kass and O'Neill, op cit., 324.
79 Ibid.
80 Ibid.
81 Ibid., 325.
82 "Israel's New Syrian View," *Time*, July 5, 1999, 44.
83 "Barak, Arafat have their first public squabble," *Milwaukee Journal-Sentinel*, August 3, 1999.

84 Before Netanyahu "suspended the deal," the Israelis carried out "only about 2%" (ibid.).

85 Ibid.

86 Ibid.

87 Ibid.

88 Ibid.

89 From an Interfaith Alliance brochure.

90 Ibid.

91 Op cit.

92 *The Deadly Embrace*, 118.

93 "Talking Peace," *Duke Magazine*, Vol. 84, No. 2, January-February 1998, 50.

Chapter 5

Israel and the Arab Countries in the Quest for Peace

This chapter will trace current relations between Israel and its Arab neighbors, Egypt, Lebanon, and Syria, and between it and Saudi Arabia, with respect to (a) prospects for peace between Israel and Syria and Lebanon, and present obstacles to its achievement; and (b) prospects for continued normalization of relations between Egypt-Jordan and Israel, which would replace the "cold peace"[1] between the former two (especially Egypt) and Israel, with a "warm peace." The "peace dividend" described in the next chapter can be enjoyed by Israel and the Arab countries provided that normal relations arise between them and continue long enough to allow for mutual respect and trust to salve the wounds of a tragic century-long conflict.

I shall begin with (a) above, where a state of belligerence still technically exists between Israel and its northern Arab neighbors, Lebanon and Syria. I shall first consider present Israeli-Lebanese relations, leading naturally to present Israel-Syria relations.

I

Israel and Lebanon
One of the many sad ironies of the long-drawn-out Arab-Israeli conflict is that Lebanon, which remained on the sidelines as Arab armies and Israel fought four bloody wars, became the stage on which Israel, the PLO, Syria, and pro-Iranian guerrillas fought their own complicated battles, and in 1978 and 1982, the victim of an Israeli invasion that reached the capital Beirut, in order to oust the PLO from Lebanon, and to drive back Hezbollah guerrillas.[2] As if that were not enough, the country almost succeeded in destroying itself in a costly and debilitating 15-year internecine war from 1975-1990. In addition, the *pax syriana* that Syria's military presence in Lebanon has brought the country[3] has been at the cost of

Lebanon's sovereignty. Israel's creation of a "security" buffer zone in south Lebanon to protect Israel's northern towns from attacks by pro-Iranian Shiite Hezbollah guerrillas has failed to give them the security they desired, but has intensified the guerrilla attacks in order to expel Israel from Lebanese soil. Since that time nearly 200 Israeli soldiers have been killed fighting Hezbollah and other guerrillas. Many more guerrillas and Lebanese civilians, including the 102 men, women, and children who had taken refuge in a UN camp, have been killed by Israeli fire in 1996, the last large scale military action in southern Lebanon by Shimon Perez's Labor government. In 1997 the Israelis lost 39 soldiers, as well as 73 soldiers en route to Lebanon "when two military helicopters crashed in February 1997."[4] Lebanese villages harboring or suspected of harboring guerrillas have been periodically pounded or destroyed by Israeli ground and air forces.

In sum, whatever "relations" can be said to exist between Israel and Lebanon are anything but peaceful ones, and there is no hope for a change for the better so long as Israel does not withdraw from the security zone, and the renegade Christian militia it created to patrol it is not disbanded.

With the guerrillas increasing military skill and effectiveness, and mounting Israeli casualties, public pressure as well as pressure from some top army men in Israel to pull out of the security zone has been building. On February 28, 1998, Netanyahu declared that his government is seriously thinking of pulling out of the security zone, saying that "he had 'no qualms' about implementing" the 1978 UN resolution" (resolution 425). That resolution called upon Israel's unconditional withdrawal from southern Lebanon and for the deployment of the Lebanese army and UN forces to ensure security along the Lebanese-Israeli border."[5]

In response to Netanyahu's suggestion, the spiritual leader of the Hezbollah guerrillas, Sheik Hassan Nasrallah, commented that "Hezbollah guerrillas will not patrol the Lebanese-Israeli border if Israel's army leaves the occupation zone it started carving into Lebanon 20 years ago."[6] These comments were the closest Nasrallah had come to addressing Israeli fears that a troop withdrawal from southern Lebanon would bring the guerrilla threat closer to the border.

Nasrallah's remarks coincided with increasing talk of an Israeli withdrawal, including UN Secretary-General Kofi Annan's discussions with Lebanese leaders in Beirut,[7] where he said that Israeli troops should be withdrawn from southern Lebanon, as required under UN Resolution 425, although he stopped short of "endorsing Syrian and Lebanese demands that the withdrawal be unconditional." He expressed the hope that Resolution 425 would be soon fully implemented. "The question is, how do you go about this? . . . Facts have been created on the ground. How could those facts impact on the implementation?"[8] Resolution 425 had passed on March 19, 1978. Under that Resolution, the UN Security Council called upon Israel to withdraw forthwith its forces from all Lebanese territory, and decided "to establish immediately under its authority a United Nations interim force for southern Lebanon for the purpose of confirming the withdrawal of Israeli forces, restoring international peace and security, and assisting the government of Lebanon in ensuring the return of its effective authority in the area."[9]

Netanyahu's insistence that the implementation of the resolution is conditional on "the necessary security safeguards"[10] being satisfied, led to the Lebanese (and Syrian) government's quick rejection of his suggestion of withdrawal, insisting on Israel's unconditional withdrawal.

Despite its quick rejection, Netanyahu's offer is important in that it did signal a significant change in Israel's military and political thinking, and the hope that the war of attrition that has gone on for so long will soon come to the end. In addition to the fact that Israel has come to recognize that "the Iranian-backed Islamic group had become a formidable foe," it is significant (especially coming from the hardline Likud government), that, "according to Israel's top official for Lebanon affairs, Israel's willingness to withdraw from southern Lebanon signaled its willingness "to modify its political goals in Lebanon." "This is a new thing," the official told an Israeli TV station. "It means that we are willing to talk today—full stop—about security." "We have gotten off the issue of peace, off the issue of normalization."[11] In other words, according to these statements, Israel's withdrawal is not conditional on the signing of a peace treaty, of normalization of relations, with Lebanon—thereby signaling a significant change in Israeli policy in place since 1985.

Lebanon's rejection of Netanyahu's suggestion clearly reflected Syria's position as much as Lebanon's, *vis-à-vis* Israel. Certainly Lebanon would be happy to regain part of its territory, and much relieved to see the disbanding of Hezbollah and an end to fighting in southern Lebanon, and the disbanding of Hezbollah. For Israel, the creation of a secure zone in southern Lebanon means, first and foremost, the disbanding of the Hezbollah guerrillas. The catch is that that is something which only Syria can presently do. As a satellite of Syria, Lebanon lacks the political power to respond to Israeli overtures and to negotiate with it in its own right, besides lacking the military power to force Hezbollah to disband. Therefore, as things stand, we have one of those recurrent "Catch-22" situations of which the history of the Arab-Israeli conflict is replete; inasmuch as Hezbollah claims as its raison d'être the expulsion of Israel from southern Lebanon. In other words, I believe that for negotiations about the security zone to succeed, Israel must withdraw and Hezbollah must simultaneously disband, provided that, at the same time, the UN is willing to beef up its international force in southern Lebanon to satisfy the Israelis: assuming that the latter, who have a history of suspicion of UN forces, agrees to that! Given the level of distrust between Israel and Syria, such simultaneous withdrawal is quite unlikely, with each party awaiting the other to go first.

As if these obstacles were not enough, negotiations (let alone agreement) about southern Lebanon cannot realistically begin without Syrian-Israeli negotiations about, if not a peaceful resolution of, the Golan dispute. Although the resolution of the "security zone" issue should go some way toward the normalization of Lebanese-Israeli relations, and may eventually include the signing of a peace treaty, it is quite doubtful in my view that that would be possible until at least a partial return of the Golan. Indeed, Syria has long insisted on the total return of the Golan Heights. Soon after taking office, Netanyahu stated that Israel will not return the Golan: at least not until trust is built between the two countries, which he equated with the establishment of a democratic regime in Syria.

Since he took office in July 1999, Ehud Barak has expressed optimism about the prospects for a resolution of the Golan Heights issue within the 15 months that he set for himself to reach peace agreements with Syria, Lebanon, and the Palestinians.[12] In line with that, President Clinton has written to Assad, expressing his confidence that Barak "was willing to hold peace talks after a three-year stalemate," and urging him to "'seize the moment of opportunity' for peace negotiations with Israel." Clinton also invited Assad to "stay in touch with him."[13]

II

Israel and Syria

Just as Israeli-occupied territory is the key to Lebanese-Israeli and Palestinian-Israeli relations, the Golan,[14] as stated above, is the (or, at least, a) key to Israeli-Syrian relations, and—in the words of one writer—is "pivotal to a solution of the Israeli-Syrian conflict, and, indeed, a *sine qua non* for peace between the two countries."[15] Since I share the widely held view that peace between Syria and Israel can only come about if Israel returns the Golan, I shall argue that Israel would gain more than it would lose in the long run, if the return of the *entire* Golan becomes necessary to end the standoff between the two countries and result in a peace treaty with adequate mutual security provisions. Such a peace treaty should increase the stability of the area and would enhance both countries' national security. I shall argue in support of this claim by addressing the main arguments of those Israelis who see the Golan as strategically crucial to their country's security and to the continued existence of the Jewish settlements that have taken root there (aside from its importance "for its regional water sources"[16]) and consequently oppose even partial withdrawal.

Muslih distinguishes three Israeli positions on the Golan, which were formulated at the time of his writing (c. 1993-1994): (a) an ambivalent position with regard to the extent of "potential withdrawal from the area"; (b) the position of those who wanted Israel to retain the Golan; and (c) the position of those who advocated an "almost total withdrawal in return for full peace."[17] The Rabin government adopted the first view; but at one point Rabin stated that the question of Israeli withdrawal would have to be determined by a plebiscite. As we saw, the Netanyahu government has adopted the second view. Since then, no negotiations between the two countries have taken place. As Muslih says, this is basically the same view held earlier by many Likud members and some Labor hard-liners since they did not trust Syria to honor peace because of the nature of its political regime and the ideology of the Baathist party.[18] The hard-liners also believe that Israel cannot afford to make a territorial compromise on grounds of security. They maintain that what threatens Israel's existence— "a small country . . . surrounded by Arab states"—is ground attack.[19] In this, as in various other respects, the current Netanyahu government hews closely to the Begin and Shamir Likud hard-line position; although the hard-liners' argument that Israel is surrounded by enemy Arab countries is no longer true, since the peace treaty with Egypt and with Jordan. The oft-repeated argument about Israel's security carried much more force prior to Egypt's and Jordan's, particularly Egypt's, peace with Israel.

The Labor Party moderates and others advocate the principle of Israel's almost complete withdrawal from the Golan "in return for total peace," while others "even call for a total withdrawal in return for total peace."[20]

Since I agree with the last group, who call for total withdrawal—if that is what it would take to have total peace between Syria and Israel—I shall consider the three assumptions that, according to Muslih, underlie the dovish view. The first assumption (1) is that in the age of missiles, "peace and security can exist without being conditional on sitting on occupied territory."[21] Since Israel is known to have missiles (leaving aside the fact that it may also have the capability of tipping these missiles with nuclear bombs) as well as American F16 and other advanced war planes that can reach any part of Syria and, indeed, any other part of the Middle East, the first assumption is well-founded. As Muslih says, for those who support the dovish view, strategic depth is irrelevant to missiles and other modern weapons. Missiles (which Syria is known to have) launched from Syria, "will not stop in the Golan."[22] (2) "This camp also assumes that Syria will not make peace without getting the Golan back.[23] That view is supported by Syria's position since Israel's conquest of the Golan in 1967.[24] (3) Finally, it is assumed that security does not lie only in territory but in "real peace, strict demilitarization, and security guarantees."[25] This assumption, like the first two, is eminently true.

Let us now turn to the arguments of those who oppose Israel's withdrawal from any part of the Golan.

As we saw, the opponents of withdrawal argue, first, that, as Muslih puts it, "the source of the threat to Israel's existence . . . is ground attack," and that "security is territory." This argument is patently unsound, for the reason General Tamir gives. His reason also applies to the first part of one of the arguments advanced by the doves who argue for only partial withdrawal; namely, that the Golan is of "such strategic value that it cannot be returned to Syria in its entirety, since, "unlike the vast Sinai Peninsula [which was returned by Israel to Egypt in its entirety]," "the Golan is only 15 to 25 kilometers from the pre-1967 Israeli border at its widest point," and overlooks "the densely populated Israeli settlements of the north." The second part of the argument is that these populated areas "contain the sources of the Jordan River." The Golan, therefore, unlike the Sinai, does not "facilitate the creation of such demilitarized areas."[26]

The conflict between Israel and Syria over the use of the waters of the Jordan River and its tributaries goes back to the creation of Israel, but intensified in the 1960s, and, by 1963, the Israeli project to divert the waters of the Jordan river to the Negev was almost complete. Although the Jordan's waters were particularly vital to Jordan and Israel, "Syria believed that its interests as a riparian state were at stake, especially because Israel sought to reconstruct a controversial track and drainage ditch . . . [in an area] believed to be the traditional source of the Jordan River."[27] Clearly, any peace agreement between Israel and Syria must attempt to provide an equitable, cooperative solution of the water problem, so that both countries, together with Jordan, share that precious and, in the area, rare commodity; just as agreement between Israel and Jordan about their water problem is urgent,[28] now that peace between them is a reality.

A second argument favoring partial withdrawal states that "disengaging Syria from the Arab-Israeli conflict justifies finding a basis for territorial compromise," with "demilitarized zones and arrangements that give Israel a basis to exercise control," particularly over "the Mount Hermon massif in the far north and the steep scalp overlooking positions of metropolitan Israel to the West," "where the headwaters of the Jordan River lie." In addition, "the Baniyas Spring, a major Jordan River source, is located on the lower slopes of the Golan."[29]

A third argument pertains to Jewish settlements on the Golan. Opposition to the dismantling of these settlements is an important consideration both for those who favor territorial compromise and those who are strongly opposed to any such compromise. However, the resolution of that issue suggested in chapter 4 in relation to the Jewish settlements on the West Bank and Gaza Strip can be similarly applied to the Jewish settlements in the Golan. As the reader may recall, I suggested that in a future Palestinian state those Jewish settlers who wish to move to Israel should receive compensation from the Palestinian state, with international aid; while those who opt to remain under Palestinian rule should be granted citizenship and enjoy the equal protection of the law, with the same civil rights as all other citizens. It is noteworthy that, as Muslih points out, a similar view is (or was) held by some Israeli doves who argued that "just as there are many Arabs living under Israeli rule, there is no reason to prevent Israelis from living under Arab [here Syrian] rule."[30]

The situation between Israel and Syria being what it is, it may well await what the historian Walid Khalidi calls "thinking the unthinkable"—the creation of a Palestinian state—for the incentive for the two countries to resolve the Golan issue. If a Palestinian state is created, Syria and Israel would come under great pressure from various quarters—Syria's President Assad from his own people and from Egypt, Jordan, and perhaps the Gulf states, and both Assad and Israel from the international community—to seek a final resolution of the Golan problem and to sign a peace treaty. That the resolution of the Palestine Problem is crucial to Syria's being amenable to negotiate peace with Israel follows from Assad's demand that, to have peace with Israel, it must withdraw to its pre-1967 borders, which means withdrawing from the West Bank and Gaza Strip as well as from southern Lebanon, not only from the Golan. In response to that, *inter alia*, the Rabin government, in its negotiations with the Syrian delegation to the peace talks, stated that peace with Israel "must entail full-fledged diplomatic, cultural, and economic relations and must not be encumbered by linkages to Palestine." No possible linkages to Palestine would remain if, in the meantime, the Palestine Problem is resolved. Similarly with the point made by Itamar Rabinovich's point as the Rabin government's ambassador to United States, that peace with Israel "must not be encumbered by linkages to . . . Lebanon."[31]

Three additional points on which Israel's official position was based were: (a) that "Syria must spell out the nature of the peace it will be willing to make with Israel before Israel defines the extent of the withdrawal it would be willing to make from the Golan; (b) an extensive security regime predicated upon mutuality and reciprocity must be established; (c) Syria must engage more in public diplomacy designed to impress and convince Arabs and Israel alike that it wants peace with Israel."[32] I believe Assad would not accept point (a), apart from the crucial fact (to which I shall return later) that the entire Golan is Syrian territory, and so, on both moral and international legal grounds, should be returned to Syria. But point (b) is clearly in the interest of both countries to implement. As to point (c), al-Assad can claim that he had engaged in lengthy public diplomacy with the U.S. secretary of state Warren Christopher during President Bill Clinton's first term of office, without that leading anywhere. In any event, as I stated under subsection I, the resolution of the Golan and Palestinian issues should facilitate speedy negotiations between Lebanon/Syria and Israel, and lead to the latter's withdrawal from southern Lebanon.

III

Israel and Egypt
Unlike Syria and Lebanon, where "land for peace" is not yet a reality, Egypt is the prime—and so far the only—successful example of the policy of land for peace. Consequently, it may be wondered why Israel has not opted for the same policy in relation to Syria and Lebanon.

The answer of course is that the Sinai desert lacked for Israel the strategic importance especially of the Golan, and had less economic value to it, despite its loss of the oil wells it had begun to exploit, and the painful dismantling of the Jewish settlements on the Egyptian side of the Red Sea, in the face of the settlers' stiff resistance. But the number of people who had to be displaced was much smaller than the number of Jewish settlers in the Golan. Finally, and most importantly, Egypt was militarily the most powerful of the Arab states in the region, and, prior to the peace treaty, the greatest threat to Israel's survival and security. It was therefore easier for Israel to give up the Sinai for the price of permanent elimination of that threat, especially as Israel gained considerable security without losing an inch of its own territory. On the other hand, Egypt's gain, apart from the boost to its national pride, has been largely military and economic, as the continuing recipient of American military and economic largesse, outlasting its temporary blackballing by the other Arab states for its separate peace with the common enemy.

After the Six Day War, Israel viewed the Sinai (as also the other occupied territories) as an "assurance of security while no plausible diplomatic settlement could offer similar guarantees. The Arabs demanded unconditional return of the occupied territories with only an end to belligerency in return, not a formal peace."[33] "Both Israel and Egypt accepted Security Council Resolution 242, calling for a 'just and lasting peace' within 'secure and recognized boundaries,' but widely divergent interpretations tended to make the resolution an additional bone of contention rather than a path to peace."[34]

After the October 1973 war, a main Israeli objective became the avoidance of "pressures for a comprehensive solution that would involve the creation of a Palestinian state and the return of territory on the eastern and northern borders."[35] A second objective was "to pull Cairo out of 'the circle of conflict' by means of a separate peace."[36] That would significantly reduce the pressure for Israel to compromise on other fronts: what in fact happened after the Egyptian-Israeli peace treaty was signed, despite President Carter's understanding that the resolution of the Palestinian problem would follow suit. Menachem Begin's interpretation was different, believing that Israel's obligations under the Camp David Accords were fulfilled by his signing the peace treaty with Egypt, although, shortly after Sadat's visit [to Jerusalem], and in order to further negotiations, Begin had presented, in a visit to Romania, an autonomy plan for the West Bank and Gaza.[37] The peace treaty gained both Egypt and Israel, American aid and political support. To Moshe Dayan, "step-by-step accords" were a means of testing Egypt's trustworthiness, providing time to monitor its compliance with the treaty's provisions.[38] This is a tactic Netanyahu has been religiously following in relation to the very modest autonomy provisions his predecessors, Rabin and Peres, had implemented in relation to the Palestinians.

IV

Israel and Jordan
The Israeli step-by-step policy that culminated in the Israeli-Egyptian peace treaty was also used in relation to Jordan; and on October 24, 1994,

King Hussein of Jordan and Yitzhak Rabin of Israel signed a peace treaty, which marked the end of a state of war going back to 1948. Earlier, on June 7, 1994, Israel and Jordan signed documents relating to "borders, security, energy, water, and the environment."[39] In addition, joint projects to promote economic growth and tourism, including trade and transportation, were also to be directly discussed the following month. Several important events paved the way for the treaty. The first was the announcement of the Oslo Accords between Israel and the PLO in September 1993. That Accord in turn was made possible, among other things, by Hussein's formally renouncing Jordan's claim of sovereignty to the West Bank territory (but not to the Muslim shrines in East Jerusalem[40]) on July 31, 1988;[41] the territory Jordan had ruled from the end of the 1948 war until 1967, when it lost it to Israel. Hussein's renunciation of Jordan's claim of sovereignty to the West Bank in favor of the Palestinians, in effect brought to an end Israel's longstanding policy of a "Jordanian Palestine" on the West Bank and Gaza Strip.

In the absence of the aforementioned two important occurrences, Jordan could not sign a peace treaty with Israel: certainly it could not earlier join in the Egyptian-Israeli peace process because of the hostility of most Arab states, as well as its own Palestinian population, toward Egypt's separate peace with Israel.[42] Only years later was Egypt allowed to rejoin the Arab League. Although the Israeli-PLO Accords fell far short of a peace settlement, they gave the "green light" to Jordan in its relations with Israel.[43] If Jordan signed a separate peace with Israel, it opened itself to possible military threats by Syria and Iraq, and to the danger of their "supporting or sponsoring domestic destabilization within Jordan."[44] Similarly, there was the danger of Saudi Arabian displeasure at the Jordanian-Israeli peace process, including the "threat of economic blackmail."[45] In fact, Jordan's Palestinian population, and most Arab states, had expressed hostility toward what they perceived as Egypt's separate peace with Israel[46] What the United States and the Gulf States saw as Jordan's siding with Iraq on the eve of, and during, the Gulf War, dramatized the extent of the economic hardships that the angered Kuwait and the Saudi monarchy could create for the Hashemite state.[47] But Hussein's stand toward Iraq during the Gulf War was tremendously popular and strengthened his legitimacy; and that encouraged the King to turn toward the revival of the Arab-Israeli peace process after the war, notwithstanding the economic and political cost to Jordan for its siding with Iraq: the expulsion of almost half a million Palestinians and Jordanians from the Gulf States and United States' cutting off its economic aid to Jordan.[48]

At the same time, Jordan moved toward political liberalization by allowing parliamentary elections and legalizing certain parties, thus strengthening the Hashemite regime despite the opposition to the treaty by Islamists in Jordan. The outspoken Islamist leader Layth Shubaylat and other critics attacked the King's peace treaty and normalization of relations with Israel, and his regime's increasing criticism of Iraq, Jordan's former ally, together with "its overt embrace of a closer strategic partnership with the United States."[49]

Ryan sums up some of the preceding factors thus: "The presence of the Israeli-PLO negotiation muted previously dominant domestic and regional constraints on the [Jordanian] regime's ability to conclude a full peace treaty [with Israel]. Second, Jordanian willingness to press further along the peace process was propelled by American political pressure coupled with economic incentives to achieve a major breakthrough on the Jordanian-Israeli track. Third, the regime had concluded that the above opportunities would lead to tangible material gains that would in turn, serve to mollify any domestic skepticism as well as outweigh any hostility from Syria."[50]

The revival of the peace process after the Gulf War enabled Jordan to reestablish some economic and political relations with the United States, but not with Saudi Arabia and the other Gulf States, and provided an incentive for it to seek a breakthrough in the peace process both for its own sake and for the economic benefits it believed would result from peace. The economic benefits were expected to mollify the regime's critics and provide the "necessary economic 'payoffs' to key constituencies—such as the business elites and the military—which provided the basis of the ruling domestic coalition on which the regime itself was based."[51]

Concerning Israel's post-Oslo "Jordanian option,"[52] Aharon Klieman writes: "Identification with the Jordanian option has represented one permanent fixture of the overall national consensus in Israel."[53] Thus "the cordiality that has marked Jordan's belated entry into peaceful relations with Israel and Israelis since 1994 has not been an insignificant factor in preserving Jordan's stock of good will among the Israeli public, and hence the residual option itself."[54] And, "geographic proximity, respective security dilemmas, shared interests [in water resources], mutual allies and opponents, pragmatic leaders willing to adopt a similar businesslike approach yielding tangible returns (plus the three assets of ambiguity, deniability, and resiliency)—repeatedly won out. These qualities invariably conduced toward fostering a supportive relationship on the ground, where it really matters most."[55] Klieman correctly adds: "Leaving aside [a] residue of nostalgic and anachronistic ideological notions of 'both banks of the Jordan' (incorporated in the Jewish homeland), when evaluated solely in terms of policy practice—deeds, rather than words—Likud-led governments have quite studiously avoided in any way consciously undermining or destabilizing King Hussein's rule. In other words, even right-wing Likud leaders belong under the loose umbrella of the pro-Jordanian consensus."[56]

More recent events, such as the streams of Israeli tourists to various Jordanian sites; Hussein's gravesite eulogy for the fallen Yitzhak Rabin in November 1995; and his participation in the Taba conference that aimed at combating terrorism, added to the very special status that all Israelis accorded Jordan and the King personally. But the Mossad's bungled and failed attempt to assassinate the leader of Hamas in Jordan strained the King's erstwhile cordial relations with the Netanyahu's government.[57]

In the immediate post-Oslo period, Hussein demonstrated his willingness to work for peace with any elected Israeli leader, and so, was "well-positioned after June [1996, when Netanyahu won the premiership] to pursue a strong working relationship with prime minister-elect Netanyahu and his Likud coalition." [58] After the Mossad incident, Netanyahu turned for a time to Egypt's Mubarak for consultations about the stalled PLO-Israeli peace process: a standoff that seemed to end with the October 1998 Wye Agreement, but was to rear its ugly head again.

V

Israel and the Arab Gulf States

Unlike the Arab states bordering Israel, Saudi Arabia and the other Gulf states lack a common border with Israel—for example, Saudi Arabia, the largest and economically and strategically most important of the Gulf States, is geographically separated from Israel by Syria and Jordan on the north—and were never directly involved in the fighting between the Arabs and Israel. In fact, except for a few recent joint economic ventures by Israel and some of the Gulf states (see chapter 6), one cannot strictly speak of relations between Israel and the Gulf States. Any "relations" (other than the ones I noted) that possibly existed have been indirect ones, through their direct economic (petrodollar), political and other relations with the other Middle East Arab states and with the West, particularly the United States. Through these relations, Israel and the Gulf states "intersected"—to borrow a metaphor from one writer on the subject[59]—with the Arab-Israeli conflict and, in that sense, with Israel.

Until the early 1970s the Gulf States, including Saudi Arabia, were essentially on the sidelines with respect to the Arab-Israeli conflict. But with the end of the security system with which the West surrounded Saudi Arabia in 1955-1956 and the Soviet Union's "virtually simultaneous appearance in Egypt, the intensification of the Arab-Israeli conflict, and the emergence of Arab nationalism as a powerful force under the leadership of Egypt's President Gamal Abdel Nasser,"[60] the conservative Saudis were alarmed. "For them, Zionism and Communism were the 'twin evils.' Because of the Arab-Israeli conflict, Arab states such as Egypt and Syria found it necessary to turn to the Soviets for arms. Many Saudi leaders concluded that, but for Israel, the Soviet Union "never would have gained a foothold in Egypt."[61] (In that belief they were clearly right.)

The Arab-Israeli dispute has "intersected" the politics of the Gulf in various ways. The first is the substantial economic assistance the Gulf States have provided to the Arab states confronting Israel, and to the PLO. "As far back as the 1950's, there was increasing pressure on Saudi Arabia, twenty years before the Arab oil embargo, to wield its oil power to put pressure on the United States and other Western countries, forcing Israel to withdraw from Arab lands." King Faisal successfully resisted this pressure until 1970 on economic and political grounds; but when the oil market changed, he saw that he could not avoid confrontation with the United States over that issue, and that his country "was in a position to undertake it."[62] But the oil embargo, in which the other Gulf OPEC states joined Saudi Arabia, did not lead to any Israeli concessions on territory but only to American anger against Arabs in general, which continued after the embargo was dropped. The Saudi demand that the United States take a "more balanced stance in relation to the Arab-Israeli conflict"[63] did not materialize. Nor did Israel withdraw from Arab lands. Abir states that although there are "conflicting reports" about the role the Saudis played in the preparation for the October 1973 war between Egypt and Syria against Israel, it is clear that Faisal won, at least for the time being, the "respect and affection" of most Arabs as a result of his "use of the 'oil weapon' during and after the . . . war, and the embargo[64] on oil exports to the United States and Holland." With the dramatic increase in the country's oil revenues, Saudi Arabia became the "financier of the Arab and Muslim worlds, thus 'buying' her peace even with the more radical Arab countries (*riyal politik*)."[65]

In the hope that war would be avoided by diplomacy, in spring 1973 Faisal warned the West that war was imminent. But his warnings went unheeded. On October 6, Egypt and Syria went to war against Israel, and two weeks later Faisal imposed the oil weapon against the United States, leading most Arabs to see it as a "victory of sorts," giving the Saudis credit for playing an "essential part" in the victory. From then on, the Saudis would not be allowed "to remain on the sidelines" [as they had been for a long time] [,] and plead that the oil weapon was a two-edged sword that should never be wielded." 66

With the end of the oil embargo in 1974, Fahd's readiness to "help maintain a regular supply of oil to the market, and to curb the rise of oil prices," led the United States to help find a solution to the Arab-Israeli conflict "acceptable to the Arabs, and help the Saudis build up their defence capabilities, through the construction of suitable military infrastructure (which the US used in 1990), . . . close relations with the United States, co-operation concerning oil supply and pricing, and Saudi involvement in negotiations relating to the settlement of the Arab-Israeli conflict, became important strands in Fahd's government after the death of Faisal."67

The second way in which, Pridham points out, the Arab-Israeli conflict "intersected" with the politics of the Gulf was by these states' becoming involved in Arab politics relating to the conflict, particularly as it affected Egypt, Jordan, Syria, and Lebanon, the four Arab states bordering Israel. Since 1973, the diplomatic initiatives under United States' sponsorship, and the 1982–1983 crisis in Lebanon, created challenges for the Gulf States they were unable to "avoid, or resolve."68 Fahd's May 1977 trip to Washington to discuss "American policy relating to the settlement of the Arab-Israeli conflict"69 was an example.

Egypt's separate peace with Israel in 1979 led to Egypt's expulsion from the Arab League, and its isolation from the rest of the Arab world, including Saudi Arabia. The frustrated Palestinians demanded that the Arab oil producing countries use their oil to further Palestinian rights. A year later Syria and Israel were embroiled in a "dangerous conflict" in Lebanon as a result of Israel's invasion of that country—a conflict that was being "fought at Lebanon's expense." Israel's continued occupation of Arab lands, including East Jerusalem, was of "particular concern to Saudis"70 because of the position the Muslim holy sites in East Jerusalem occupied in Islam.

Israel withdrew from the Sinai as a result of the Egyptian-Israeli peace accords, but continued to occupy the Golan, the West Bank and Gaza Strip, and southern Lebanon. In an attempt to find a political solution to the continuing Arab-Israeli conflict, Fahd announced an eight-point plan on August 7, 1981, involving Israel's returning these territories as part of a comprehensive peace settlement. The principles included "Israeli withdrawal from all the Arab territories occupied in 1967, including Arab Jerusalem; Removal of the settlements established by Israel in the Arab territories after 1967; Guaranteeing the freedom of worship and religious practices for all religions in the holy places; Asserting the rights of the Palestinian people to return to their homes and compensating those who do not wish to return; . . . Establishing an independent Palestinian state with Jerusalem as its capital; Affirming the right of all the states in the region to live in peace; Guaranteeing the implementation of these principles by the United Nations or some of its member states."[71]

According to Abir, the Fahd plan met with Syrian and PLO opposition, and was abandoned, replaced by "a watered-down resolution adopted at the 1982 Fez summit."[72] But, in fact, the principles adopted at that summit, with slight stylistic differences, were almost identical to the eight points of the Fahd plan. Among other things, the Fez plan stated that the principles adopted were based on the "plan of President Habib Bourguiba, which is based on international legitimacy, as the foundation for solving the Palestinian question and the plan of His Majesty King Fahd ibn 'Abd al-'Aziz which deals with peace in the Middle East."[73] It is also noteworthy that the words, "reaffirmation of the Palestinian people's right to self-determination and the exercise of its imprescriptible and inalienable national rights," in the Fez plan, were immediately followed with, "under the leadership of the Palestine Liberation Organization, its sole and legitimate representative."[74]

The third way in which the Arab-Israeli conflict has intersected with the politics of the Gulf, Pridham observes, is that the "Gulf states have faced an indirect set of challenges from Israel, which is itself concerned to prevent the consolidation of a firm anti-Israeli bloc in the peninsula. Direct Israeli involvement in the peninsula has been small: some arms to the Yemeni royalists in 1963, an arms smuggling arrangement with a minor prince in Ajman (UAE), the odd threat to South Yemen over passage through the Bab al-Mandab straits. Fourth, while it has not carried out direct military attacks on the Gulf states, even though few can doubt its ability to do so, Israel has pursued a Gulf policy in two central regards: one by pressure on the US and Europe to prevent arms going to Gulf states, and the other, support for what it considers to be influential non-Arab states that can offset the oil-production of the peninsula—Ethiopia, until 1977, and Iran."[75] And, during the Reagan administration's covert operations in Nicaragua against the Marxist rebels, Israel covertly smuggled arms to Iran.

To sum up. The chapter traced current and, to a lesser extent, relations between Israel and its Arab neighbors, and between it and Saudi Arabia, with respect to, first, the prospects for peace between Israel and Syria-Lebanon, and present obstacles to its achievement. Second, the prospects for continued normalization of relations between Israel and Egypt and Jordan. Since the most problematic relations have been between Israel and Syria, and, largely as a result, between Israel and Lebanon, special attention was paid, in the sections on Israel and Syria, and Israel and Lebanon, to (a) the Syrian-Israeli dispute over the Golan Heights, and (b) the Lebanese-Israeli conflict over Israel's "security zone" in southern Lebanon, and the latter's growing interest in withdrawing from it, provided certain security measures are set in place to protect its northern areas bordering on Lebanon. It was emphasized that the resolution of the Syrian-Israeli dispute over the Golan is the key to the resolution of the security zone dispute between Lebanon and Israel.

Finally, the section on Israeli-Saudi relations traced the indirect relations between the two countries through Saudi Arabia's direct economic and political relations with the other Middle Eastern Arab countries and with the U.S. Reference was also made to the various ways in which the Arab-Israeli conflict "intersected" with the politics of the Gulf States in general.

Notes

1. A cold peace of a much less severity than in the case of Egypt and Israel existed between Jordan and the Netanyahu government, ever since the Mosad's aborted assassination attempt of Hamas' leader in Jordan in 1998 (see later).

2. The Islamic guerrilla organization, Hezbollah or "Party of God," was funded from Iran during the 1980s and 1990s. It originated in Iran as an "extremist movement within Shi'ia Islam in support of Ayatollah Khomeini's regime. . . . With the Syrian army's takeover of much of Lebanon, Hezbollah's activities were curtailed by the early 1990's" (*Compton's Interactive Encyclopedia*, 1996). But the Encyclopedia is in error in calling Hezbollah a terrorist organization; since it mainly consists of freedom fighters who have been directing most of their attacks against the Israeli army. (See my *The Morality of Terrorism*, chapter 5.)

3. William Harris, *Faces of Lebanon* (Princeton, NJ, 1997) writes on page 58: "The 1991 Gulf war and the end of the Cold War created enough of a Syrian-American-Saudi convergence in the early 1990s for the Syrian Ba'thists to shackle Beirut to their own agenda." But he underestimates al-Asad when he adds: "However, with its diverse population of two million people, Beirut is too complex and too used to multiplicity of influence to be caged for very long by a small and unstable power like Ba'thist Syria."

4. "Netanyahu signals Israel may be willing to withdraw from Lebanon," *Milwaukee Journal Sentinel*, March 2, 1998.

5. According to a poll in the Israeli newspaper *Maariv* toward the end of November 1998, "40% of Israelis support a unilateral withdrawal, up from only 16% in February 1997. The survey was conducted among 560 adults and had a margin of error of 4.5 percentage points." (*Milwaukee Journal-Sentinel*, November 28, 1998).

6. Whether that means that Hezbollah would not attack northern Israeli villages is, however, unclear.

7. *Milwaukee Journal Sentinel*, March 22, 1998.

8. Ibid.

9. *Arab-Israeli Conflict and Conciliation, A Documentary History*, Bernard Reich, ed. (Westport, CT, 1995), 146.

10. Ibid.

11. Ibid.

12. See, for example, "Israel's New Syrian View[.] Ehud Barak is plotting a big leap toward peace. The surprise jumping-off point: Damascus," *Time*, July 5, 1999, 44.

13 *Milwaukee Journal-Sentinel*, July 27, 1999.

14 The Golan is a mountainous plateau, averaging 1000 meters, with an area of 1750 square kilometers. On June 9-10, 1967, during the Six Day War, Israel captured about 1250 square kilometers of the area. As a result of the Syrian-Israeli disengagement agreement, a year after the 1973 war, about 100 square kilometers were returned to Syria. The Golan is 65 kilometers long, north to south, and varies from 12 to 25 kilometers east to west. Its strategic importance is seen from the fact that the Israeli army is 35 kilometers from Damascus, while the Syrian army is 250 kilometers from Tel Aviv. The Golan is also important for its water resources. (Muhammad Muslih, "The Golan: Israel, Syria, and Strategic Calculations," *From Wars toward Peace in the Arab-Israeli Conflict, 1969-1993*, vol. 4, Ian S. Lustick, ed. (New York and London, 1994), 253.

15 Ibid., 243.

16 Ibid.

17 Ibid., 254.

18 Ibid., 255.

19 Ibid.

20 Ibid., 256.

21 Ibid. This assumption—or argument—is made by Avraham Tamir, "a retired general and a director-general of the Israeli Foreign Ministry when Shimon Peres was foreign minister" (ibid., 256).

22 Ibid., 257.

23 Ibid., 256.

24 A similar point is made by Helena Cobban in *The Superpowers and the Syrian-Israeli Conflict* (New York, 1991). For example, she writes that resolving the Golan issue is "a necessary first step to bring the Israeli-Syrian dispute back to the negotiating table" (ibid., 149).

25 Ibid.

26 Ibid., 254.

27 Ibid., 252.

28 See Section IV, on Israeli-Jordanian relations.

29 Ibid., 253.

30 Ibid., 255. Unfortunately, Israeli Arabs do not enjoy equal rights with their Jewish compatriots, but are second-class citizens.

31 Ibid., 254.

32 Ibid.

33 Tony Armstrong, *Breaking the Ice* [n.p.], 1993), 33.

34 Ibid., 54.

35 Ibid., 89.

36 Ibid., 90.

37 Ibid., 123. When Anwar Sadat went on his historic mission to Jerusalem, he was willing to "offer full normalization in return for full withdrawal and Palestinian self-rule in the West Bank and the Gaza Strip." However, the "Israelis would not move from their adamant refusal to relinquish all territories and continued to refuse full Palestinian autonomy in the occupied territories, let alone a Palestinian state" (ibid). Again, each step in the step-by-step process in Israeli-Egyptian negotiations was itself an Israeli "tactic to keep the peace process alive without making concessions about the West Bank or the Palestinians"(ibid). Besides its use of similar tactics, which Armstrong, following Charles Osgood, calls "Gradual Reciprocation in Tension Reduction" (ibid., 23), in its peace negotiations with Jordan, Israel has used them in relation to the peace process with the Palestinians.

38 Ibid., 90.

39 Curtis R. Ryan, "Jordan in the Middle East Peace Process: From War to Peace with Israel," *The Middle East Peace Process: Interdisciplinary Perspectives*, Ilan Peleg, ed. (Albany, NY, 1998), 189.

40 Concerning the Muslim shrines, Hussein stated: "To us, the Hashemites, Jerusalem has been an eternal trust," "consecrated by Jordanian blood" (ibid., 189).

41 *Arab-Israeli Conflict and Conciliation, a Documentary History*, Bernard Reich, ed. (Westport, CT, 1995), 199. And in 1994, Hussein rejected the idea of Palestinian statehood through "confederation" with Jordan.

42 Ryan, op. cit., 163.

43 Ibid.

44 Ibid.

45 Ibid., 163-164.

46 Ibid., 163.

47 Ibid.

48 Ibid., 167.

49 Ibid., 174.

50 Ibid., 165.

51 Ibid., 168.

52 "Israel's Jordanian Option: A Post-Oslo Reassessment," *The Middle East Peace Process, Interdisciplinary Perspectives*, 179-195.

53 Ibid., 182.

54 Ibid., 183.

55 Ibid.

56 Ibid., 183.

57 Ibid., 192. But since the accession of King Abdallah II to Jordan's throne following his father's recent death, Jordanian-Israeli relations have been, in a sense, on hold.

58 Ibid., 192.

59 *The Arab Gulf and the Arab World*, B.R. Pridham, ed. (London, 1988), 102.

60 William B. Quandt, *Saudi Arabia in the 1980s, Foreign Policy, Security, and Oil* (Washington, D.C., 1981), 4.

61 Ibid.

62 Mordecai Abir, *Saudi Arabia, Government, Society and the Gulf Crisis* (London, 1993), 66.

63 Ibid.

64 Ibid.

65 Ibid.

66 William B. Quandt, op. cit., 20.

67 Ibid., 67.

68 Pridham, op. cit., 102.

69 Abir, op. cit., 75.

70 Quandt, op. cit., 5.

71 *Arab-Israeli Conflict and Conciliation, A Documentary History*, Bernard Reich, ed. (Westport, CT, 1995), 174.

72 Abir, op. cit., 127.

73 Reich, op. cit., 180.

74 Ibid. Article (4) reads as follows: "The reaffirmation of the Palestinian people's right to self-determination and the exercise of its imprescriptible and inalienable national rights under the leadership of the Palestine Liberation Organization, its sole and legitimate representative, and the indemnification of all those who do not desire to return" (ibid., 180).

75 Pridham, op cit., 102. That included covert arms smuggling to Iran during the Iraq-Iran war under the Reagan administration.

Chapter 6

The Peace Dividend

I

During the past 50 years, one who had the welfare of the Arab people at heart would not have failed to hope that the Arab countries would rise to the greatest external challenge they have faced in a long time, by responding creatively to the existence of Israel in their midst, especially after their failed attempts to prevent it from being born, and, later, to continue to exist. But that hope was continually dashed to the ground. In vain one waited for that response as the 1967 and the 1973 wars were fought and lost, and (aside from Egypt's bold move in 1979), from then to the present. By a "creative response" on the Arabs' part I mean their transcending the humiliation and pain of their military defeats and territorial losses by focusing their energies on internal economic, political, and social change and reform; by resolutely striving to improve the standard of living of their peoples, and empowering them by respecting their human rights and according them political and civil liberties and rights; thereby helping them achieve a better individual and collective life. One also waited in vain for the dawning of a new cultural era: for the intellectual, cultural, and artistic renaissance that Arab intellectuals presaged in the early decades of the century, and which some believed did take place after the Arabs gained independence from their colonial masters. One waited, with growing impatience and frustration, as the "rebirth" failed to materialize, the Arab Dawn failed to appear. One came to see the vaunted Arab Awakening more as the promise, if not the illusion, of an awakening than an actual reality.

The rise of Arab nationalism in this century, detailed by George Antonius in *The Arab Awakening*, did not usher in a rebirth of creativity in the literary, artistic, scientific, and philosophical fields comparable in any degree to the Golden Age of Islam in the Near East in Medieval times, or in

Spain during the Arab conquest, until the fall of Granada in 1496. Nor have the Middle Eastern Arab states, with the exception of the oil rich Gulf states, met the challenge by concerted efforts to bring about a wider and fairer distribution of their economic resources—however meager in some instances—so as to raise the general standard of living. Nor have there been significant attempts to bring about fundamental political reforms, to steer the Arab countries away from their traditional authoritarian, rigidly hierarchical, and patriarchal institutional structures toward liberalism and democracy.

Until fairly recently, the Arabs' political/military response to the challenge of Israel's existence has been, as we know, mainly negative, and included, among other things, the unleashing of the scourge of terrorism. Except for the Palestinians' nascent democracy in the management of their economic, educational, social, and cultural affairs in the difficult circumstances of Israeli occupation, we have not seen much evidence of a more positive, creative response to Israel's existence and dynamism.

A noteworthy exception to the preceding has been the rise of Palestinian and other Arab nationalistic poetry, fiction, and painting: an art of protest against the occupier and an affirmation of Palestinian identity and the quest for national freedom and self-determination. Higher education and scientific research have continued in the region's universities, outside the occupied territories plagued by continual Israeli closings. But except for Iraq, where a significant amount of research was directed to military ends, including the stockpiling of chemical and biological weapons and the race to create nuclear weapons, scientific research has proceeded in the academic world independently of the Arab-Israeli conflict. Indeed, the Iraqi gearing of scientific research and technology to the arms race with Israel, and Syria's and Egypt's arms race with Israel (the latter before the Camp David Accords), have been a major destabilizing element in the Arab states' response to Israel. The same has been true of Israel's military buildup and military action *vis-à-vis* the Arabs.[1]

But the subject of this chapter is not so much the Arabs countries' past failure to transcend the tragedy of Palestine by a range of positive responses to it but, rather, the prospect of the peace dividend (to borrow a popular American phrase in the aftermath of the cold war) that can and should accrue to both Arabs and Israelis from a peaceful and just resolution of the Arab-Israeli conflict. To that peace dividend I shall turn in Section II. Before that, in Section II, I shall discuss certain claims about the "peace dividend"—the modicum of economic cooperation between Israel and the Arab countries—and the relation between such regional economic cooperation and the reduction of the regime of conflict between Arabs and Israelis.

II

In "The Peace Dividend, The Economy of Israel and the Peace Process,"[2] Ofira Seliktar examines the claim that economic prosperity ameliorates "the nationalist, zero-sum perspectives that belligerents have developed over the course of the conflict."[3] She tests that idea by analyzing the economic benefits realized by Israel and various Arab countries, from the current peace process, taking Israel as the focal point of her study.[4] In the course of her examination, she also briefly considers the idea of Arab-Israeli Common Market, and regards it as one long term possibility among others.

As one might expect, Seliktar has no difficulty in demonstrating that, through the "dismantling of the Arab boycott regime and decline in the level of regional political risk," Israel has dramatically benefitted, directly, and—especially—indirectly; e.g., as a result of increased foreign direct investments and portfolio investment. And although "in the short term, the direct benefit of regional collaboration and bilateral linkage" between Israel and the Arab countries is "more limited," she believes that it is "potentially substantial in the medium and long terms."[5]

In the case of the Middle East Arab countries the situation has been, on the whole, quite otherwise, for two basic reasons. First, these countries, Seliktar argues, "lag far behind Israel to provide a natural market for her goods and services [and we may add, 'and vice versa']," and second, "these economic disparities feed into the Arab fears of economic domination"[6] by Israel.

The actual results of the peace process, in terms of Israeli-Arab trade relations, have been disappointing; although Seliktar mentions four short-term plans for regional cooperation that have come about so far. These include the environment, water projects, tourism, and transportation.[7] The most important benefit of these ventures is to create new and more positive perceptions among former adversaries as well as new mechanisms for normal international interaction. Second, "economic prosperity is said to ameliorate the nationalist, zero-sum perspectives that belligerents have developed over the course of the conflict."[8] As I said, she tests this idea by analyzing the economic benefits realized by Israel and various Arab countries from the current peace process.[9]

Trade between Israel and Egypt has been extremely modest (around $40 million per annum). By contrast, trade between Israel and Algeria "was expected to increase to $1 billion over the next few years."[10] Two members of the Gulf Cooperation Council, Oman and Qatar, have allowed Israel to "operate trade missions," and a project to produce liquified natural gas for the two countries was to be implemented by a U.S. corporation for Qatar and Israel. The most advanced economic relations have been between Israel and Jordan, with various bilateral projects being considered. They include tourism, transportation, and energy. The latter includes plans for the "Red Sea–Dead Sea Canal," which would "generate electricity and desalinate water for both countries."[11]

Economic, especially labor, relations between Israel and the West Bank and Gaza Strip have not changed dramatically since Palestinian autonomy, and some observers "worry that the vastly more developed Israeli economy may stunt Palestinian growth, [leaving] the Palestinian entity overshadowed and dependent on its more powerful neighbor (Avineri 1994)."[12] This worry is more than justified, and emphatically calls for substantial, long-range Arab and international (if not also Israeli) economic and technological aid to the future Palestinian state, to supplement the international aid that the autonomous territories are presently receiving or have been recently pledged, to minimize or eliminate these deleterious effects.

However important the economic benefits of bilateral and regional economic relations and cooperation between Israel and the Arab countries at present may be, such relations and cooperation would be even more important, if, as claimed, the cooperation reduces conflict in international relations, by providing an "opportunity to develop confidence building measures, . . . which create new and more positive perceptions among former adversaries as well as new mechanisms for normal international interaction. Second, economic prosperity is said to ameliorate the nationalist, zero-sum perspectives that belligerents have developed over the course of the conflict.[13]

According to its proponents, the creation of a Middle Eastern Common Market, like the "West European model, . . . would achieve genuine integration and virtually eliminate the chances of conflict."[14] Others have called for the "European Common Market to form an economic union with the Middle East. Indeed, the European Commission proposed on October 19, 1994 a broad economic and security plan for North Africa/ Middle East." The plan would create a forty country FTA of some 800 million people by the turn of the century."[15] The larger union would focus less on Arabs' and Israelis' immediate needs, but a third-party's presence would be an advantage in reducing conflict. "According to Alfred Tovias (1992, 127[16]), if perceived as a neutral party, the EC could dominate cooperative ventures and 'provide partial insurance against the other side deciding to dissociate'."[17]

As Seliktar observes, there are economic and psychological obstacles to the creation of a Middle Eastern Common Market. First is the Arab states' "bloated public sector, central domination, and almost xenophobic restriction on foreign trade and investment," and the consequent absence of "market-oriented reforms, including large scale privatization of the public sector."[18] Second, "Arab fears of Israeli economic domination" because of the economic disparity between Israel and the Arab states and the "residue of suspicion left by the culture of conflict (Tovias 1992). As a result, most Arab spokesmen have rejected the idea of a common market and advocated, instead, the strengthening of ties among the Arab countries."[19]

Like Seliktar, I believe that the Middle Eastern Common Market, or an extended European Common Market that includes North Africa and the Middle East, is a long term possibility; and like the latter's proponents, I believe that its free trade area would provide the "partial insurance" Tovias envisages but which a Middle Eastern Common Market would lack as long as the factors Seliktar notes persist.

It must be added, as Seliktar does, that regional economic cooperation has its limits in terms of reducing a regime of conflict. It is clear from her analysis that economic cooperation is just one important conflict-reducing factor. Regional intellectual, scientific, cultural, and artistic interaction and cooperation, which involve personal interaction and cooperation, are, in my view, also quite important in that regard.

In the last section of her article, Seliktar asks whether the peace dividend that has, so far, resulted from the Arab-Israeli peace process, will generate more peace. Although she does not directly answer the question, one can gather from what she says that, provided a certain condition is satisfied in the coming years, she believes that the peace dividend will work effectively. The condition in question is the even distribution of the economic peace dividend among the parties, which has not transpired so far, particularly as regards the Palestinians. Instead, the meager dividend they have so far received [20] has made Palestinians continuously skeptical of the peace process, and generated support for radical groups who are opposed to any negotiations with Israel.[21] In addition, the Israeli government's punitive measures "only increased the appeal of such political extremists. Moreover, the terrorist campaign waged by Palestinian radicals, and especially the highly traumatic bombings in Jerusalem and Tel Aviv [in 1996], . . . increased security considerations among Israelis.

Under such generalized perceptions of threat, economic considerations are inevitably pushed backstage in voters' minds."[22] She concludes that the "1996 elections in Israel demonstrated the limits of the purported relations between peace, economic prosperity and the CBMs."[23]

Seliktar is clearly correct that security considerations place a limit on the extent to which economic relations and cooperation, and economic benefits, can reduce interstate conflict. But the fact that the Arab countries and, especially the Palestinians, have so far reaped little economic benefit from the so-far-brief peace process means that the present Middle East cannot serve to provide either logically adequate support for, or adequate illustration of, the general thesis that bilateral or multilateral economic relations and cooperation can and do reduce a regime of conflict between states.

Seliktar correctly concludes that,

> With all its obvious merits, the market rationality on which the [economic] "peace dividend" theory is based has always faced a tough challenge in the Middle East. In spite of the current setback [prior to the Wye Agreement], the last few years presented the first genuine opportunity for Israel and her Arab neighbors to join the global economic order and build a stable peace in the region.[24]

With this I turn to a consideration of various intellectual, scientific, artistic, and other cultural dividends that, it is hoped, will accrue to Israel, the Arab countries, and the Palestinians, over and above the dividends of economic cooperation, once a comprehensive Arab-Israeli peace is finally realized.

III

It is not, I believe, unreasonable or visionary to suppose that the end of Arab-Israeli hostilities, and the establishment of a stable peace in the Middle East, can and should bring significant benefits to the entire troubled region; starting with the slow healing of the wounds and the gradual dissipation of the mutual hatreds and distrusts, as new generations of Palestinians and Israeli Jews appear on the scene. The signing of a comprehensive peace between Arabs and Israel, including the creation of an independent Palestinian state; the opening of the borders between the Arab countries and Israel;[25] and the establishment of diplomatic and other normal relations between them, should bear the sweet fruits of peace.

The following are chief among these fruits or possible benefits of peace that I envision.

Arab terrorism against Israel and its supporters and friends, with its many destructive consequences, has been a major chapter in the violent Arab conflict with Israel since the 1970s. It is therefore not inappropriate to start with the effect, on terrorism, of a comprehensive peace treaty between Israel and all its Arab neighbors. With the creation of an independent Palestinian state—which Arafat has been calling for, and which appears to be strongly desired at least by a majority of Palestinians in West Bank and Gaza Strip as well—we should expect a very significant decrease in terrorism against Israel, by such militant groups as Hamas and Islamic Jihad. If so, no significant terrorist attempts to infiltrate Israel from the Palestinian state would be likely to occur; particularly if the provisions I envisaged in chapter 3 are implemented. Whatever terrorist activity occurs would take place without the knowledge—certainly without the blessing—of the Palestinian government or of the majority of Palestinians citizens. It would even be true of any terrorism from across the Lebanese border, since complete Israeli withdrawal from the (whole or part of the) Golan Heights and from Southern Lebanon would be part of the comprehensive peace treaty. In short, as in all other cases of terrorism in the world, present or past, the loss or absence of popular support for Arab terrorism would eventually lead to its demise.[26]

Increasing normalization of commercial and other economic relations between the Arabs and Israel, including joint economic ventures, should result from the lifting of the Arab economic boycott of Israel and the opening of the borders between the Arab countries and Israel. That process could eventually include economic ties and joint ventures between Palestinians in the new state and Arab Israelis in Israel, and other forms of Palestinian-Jordanian-Syrian and other Arab-Israeli economic cooperation. The economic relations could gradually extend to North Africa: not just to Egypt, the most obvious example, but also to Algeria, Tunisia, and Morocco. In fact, I dare to dream of the day in the next century when a Middle Eastern and North African Common Market, similar to the European Common Market, embracing Israel and most or all of the Middle East and North African Arab states, would become a reality.

A further economic benefit of major importance could accrue from cooperative bilateral and multilateral agreements between the Arab states, Turkey, and Israel concerning the judicious use and more equitable distribution of the scarce water resources in the predominantly agricultural Near East. The creation of joint desalination programs to increase the supply of water for human consumption, which may otherwise be too expensive, may become economically feasible.

Closely related to the region's overall economic development, the Arab countries can significantly benefit from Israel's advanced scientific and technological know-how; provided that it is drawn on with due sensitivity to environmental concerns to prevent further damage to the ecology in Arab countries as a result of industrialization. The exigencies of division of labor as well as environmental concerns would naturally favor the region's reliance, in the main, on Israeli industry and technology already in place for modern industrial and technological products, supplemented by imports from Japan, Europe, and the U.S. The Arab countries of the Fertile Crescent (with more efficient modern but ecologically sound agricultural methods learned from Israel as well as from the West) would continue to be the region's main breadbasket. Regional cooperation to prevent the further deterioration of the natural environment would be an important added benefit for the human inhabitants and for the rest of Nature.

With the opening up of borders, travel between the Arab countries and Israel could in time become a reality, ending the present anomalous situation. In the case of Egypt, travel between it and Israel could become a two-way street rather than, as it now is, only in one direction.

The peace dividend should include the elimination of an important source of inter-Arab political and military friction due to their different geopolitical, territorial, and military interests and ambitions; especially frictions between Syria, Iraq, Egypt, and Jordan but also between them and the more pro-American Gulf States. I have in mind here inter-Arab differences and conflicts caused by their differing perceptions and suspicions of Israel's economic, political, and military interests and ambitions in the region; consequently, their differing policies *vis-à-vis* the West, particularly the U.S. Recall, for instance, Egypt's ostracism by the other Arab states after its peace treaty with Israel, and the Gulf states' current stand toward Iraq.

The elimination of the frictions and dissensions among the Arab states *vis-à-vis* Israel would clearly leave other significant ideological, political, and territorial sources of traditional Arab disunity and rivalry unresolved. Therefore, the end of the Arab-Israeli conflict is unlikely, in and by itself, to bring the Arab countries politically closer together, toward some kind of eventual political unity, such as a federation. But as I said earlier, a Middle Eastern Common Market which includes Israel, or an extended European–Middle Eastern Common Market, could become, as it has in Western Europe, an important basis for, and a bridge to, possible political unity in the future.

The establishment of cultural exchanges between Israeli and Arab scientists, medical researchers, scholars, intellectuals, and artists would be salutary for all concerned, not least to the Arabs, who can find stimulation in, and utilize, the advances in Israeli scientific and medical research, and in intellectual and artistic achievement.

The end of the Arab-Israeli conflict should substantially decrease the economically draining and politically and militarily destabilizing arms race between the Arab countries and Israel. The end of the arms race should not only reduce the probability of future wars (above all, of wars with weapons of mass destruction[27]) between the Arabs and Israel. The huge amounts of money saved from the very significant decrease in arms purchases, wisely used, should help raise the standard of living of the region's impoverished masses, strengthen the educational systems, and help provide comprehensive health care. Not least, it may provide needed public financial assistance to scholarly, medical, and scientific research, and to artistic endeavors.

Finally, one of the greatest benefits of the end of the Arab-Israeli conflict, for Israel and not only for the Arab countries, could be the Arab countries' move toward democracy. Because of its special importance in relation to the Arab World, both in its own right and in relation to the Arab-Israeli conflict (including Arab terrorism), the next, final chapter of this book will be devoted to this question. As I shall argue there, the absence of political democracy is the deepest root-cause of the Arab Middle East's endemic instability and turmoil: possibly including the continuance of the Arab-Israeli conflict.

The preceding crucial issue directly relates to the view of some Middle Eastern scholars that continued political liberalization and democratization in the Arab World may reduce the likelihood of armed conflict between Arabs and Israelis, and would itself have ". . . a positive impact on efforts to resolve the Arab-Israeli conflict."[28] The reader may recall here my speculation in chapter 6 that a main reason for the Palestinians' rejection of the Partition Plan in 1947–1948 may have been the absence of free Palestinian political expression and the arbitrary way in which the then-Palestinian leaders decided the fate of the people as a whole by failing to give them an understanding of and an opportunity to decide their future themselves.

To sum up. The chapter opened with a brief description of the Arabs' failure, with some noteworthy exceptions, to transcend the Palestine tragedy and to meet creatively the challenge of Israel's existence, during the past half century. That led to one of the two main themes considered in the chapter: the prospects for the "peace dividend" that can, and should, accrue to Arabs and Israelis, from a peaceful and just resolution of the Arab-Israeli conflict. Section III outlined the author's vision of that peace dividend. Earlier, in Section II, the discussion turned to the question of whether economic prosperity decreases the likelihood of conflict between belligerents, as some scholars maintain. In an article titled "The Peace Dividend," Ofir Seliktar finds confirmation, in Israel's case, for that claim, and demonstrates the direct and indirect economic benefits that country has realized from foreign (non-Arab) direct investments and portfolio investment, as a result of the recent Arab-Israeli peace process. She also describes the modest (or relatively modest) peace dividend that has accrued to Egypt, Jordan, and the Palestinians through trade, tourism, etc., with Israel, and the promise of mutual benefit from the recent bilateral economic agreements between Israel and Jordan, and between Israel and a number of other Arab states.

The following are the various kinds of benefits the present author hoped would accrue to the region as a whole, from the peaceful resolution of the Arab-Israeli conflict: significant decrease in Palestinian and other Arab terrorism; increased normalization of commercial and economic relations, including joint ventures, between the Arabs and Israel, and the eventual creation of a Middle Eastern and North African Common Market or an extended European Common Market embracing the entire Middle East; economic benefits of bilateral and multilateral agreements between the Arab states, Turkey, and Israel, for judicious and more equitable distribution of the scarce water resources, and the creation of joint desalination projects; the further economic development of Arab countries that can result from the drawing on Israel's advanced scientific and technological know-how—but with due sensitivity to the region's environmental concerns; trade and tourism between Israel and all the Arab countries, that should result from the opening of all borders between them; with the end of the Arab-Israeli conflict, the reduction of friction or tensions between the Arab countries stemming from their differences and disagreements regarding Israel; establishment of cultural exchanges between Israeli and Arab scientists, medical researchers, scholars, intellectuals, and artists; substantial decrease of the economically draining and politically and militarily destabilizing arms race between Arabs and Israel; and, finally, the Arab countries' hoped-for move toward political liberalization (or further liberalization) and democracy, which would benefit the Arab masses and promise a regime of stable and lasting peace in the region.

Notes

1. For a study of the arms race in the Middle East, see *A Compassionate Peace*, Chapter 7.

2. *The Middle East Peace Process, Interdisciplinary Perspectives*, Ilan Peleg, ed. (Albany, NY, 1998), 223–235.

3. Ibid., 223.

4. Ibid., 224.

5. Ibid.

6. Ibid., 231. This has led some Arab spokesmen to reject the idea of a Middle East Common Market, embracing Israel and the Arab countries. (See later.)

7. Ibid., 229.

8. Ibid., 223.

9. Ibid., 224.

10. Ibid., 233.

11. Ibid., 232.

12. Ibid. Schlomo Avineri, "Sidestepping Dependency," *Foreign Affairs* 73 (4), 1994: 12–15.

13. Ibid., 223.

14. Ibid., 228.

15. Ibid., 229.

16. Alfred Tovias, "The EC's Contribution to Peace and Prosperity in the Mediterranean and the Middle East: Some Proposals," *The Jerusalem Journal of International Relations* 14, 1992: 123–132.

17. Seliktar, ibid., 229.

18. Ibid., 228.

19. Ibid., 229. Even that objective would be difficult to achieve until the political rivalries and suspicions among the Arab countries themselves are overcome.

20. Similarly with the meager economic dividend of the Arab countries, described in Section I.

21. When Sheik Yassin was released from an Israeli jail, he offered a conditional truce with Israel. But that did not constitute an offer for negotiation.

22 Ibid., 234. This, we might repeat, is all the more reason why a much more positive economic and political Israeli policy, e.g., in relation to the West Bank and Gaza Strip, including, most importantly, speedy Palestinian statehood, is urgently needed.

23 Ibid. Thus, "the borders [between Israel and the Palestinian Authority] are bitterly contested and the Palestinians have not [we should add, 'quite'] evolved into a cohesive national agency. Most important, the pervasive threat of terrorism has had a devastating impact on the collective psychology of Israeli Jews. Under such circumstances, the tenuous confidence building measures are likely to crumple and the imperatives of economic rationality can easily be overruled" (ibid., 235).

24 Ibid.

25 An end to hostilities even between Iraq and Israel, and the normalization of relations between the two countries some time during the twenty-first century, cannot be completely ruled out, if (but it is a big "if") a democratic government replaces or follows President Saddam Hussein's present regime. The possibility of democracy there would depend in good measure on factors considered in the next chapter.

26 See, for instance, Leonard B. Weinberg and Paul Davis, *Introduction to Political Terrorism* (New York, 1989), chapter 7, especially 194f. Some examples mentioned by the authors on p. 194 are Armenian terrorism and French Quebec terrorism as well as the Red Brigade terrorism in Italy. I quote: "Defeat is not the only or even the most frequent way in which terrorist groups have come to an end. Another is through a process of *backlash*. In some cases, as with Armenian communities in exile and French-speaking Canadians in Quebec, the ethnic groups whose causes the terrorists have sought to lead have displayed revulsion at the atrocities that were committed in their name. The process of de-legitimizing the terrorists among their ostensible constituency has also been at work in Italy" (ibid., 194. Italics in original). And so on. The authors go on to call attention to "*burnout* or disintegration for reasons that are largely internal to the organization" (ibid. Italics in original). Earlier, on p.112-113, the authors note the transformation and the end of terrorism in the case of the Irgun, "as a branch of revisionist Zionism, which, after Israel's achievement of independence, became transformed into a political party." The same could very conceivably happen to the PLO if Palestinians achieve statehood. Since Arafat's public renunciation of terrorism on December 4, 1988, and August 1990, Fatah terrorism has ended, and, as is common knowledge, the PLO has become the ruling national authority in the autonomous regions of the West Bank and Gaza Strip.

27 The UN's and the U.S.'s attempts to eliminate Iraq's weapons of mass destruction and the degradation of its capability to produce such weapons anew, if they were to continue in the future, should lead Israel (a) to gradually eliminate its arsenal of nuclear weapons, to provide an incentive to any country in the region that desires to develop nuclear, chemical, or biological weapons as a putative deterrent against what they might perceive as possible future Israeli expansionist ambitions; and lead it (b) to sign the international nonproliferation treaty. That

should provide an incentive to Egypt and to other Arab countries that have to date not signed the treaty, to follow suit. The latest round of dangerous nuclear contretemps between India and Pakistan should be timely warning in this regard. As for Iran, U.S. pressure on Russia needs to continue in hopes of preventing Iran from acquiring weapons of mass destruction. If Iran does acquire such weapons, it would give Israel an excuse if not a reason for maintaining or even enhancing its arsenal of nuclear weapons.

28 Mark Tessler and Marilyn Gorbschmidt, "Democracy in the Arab World and the Arab-Israeli Conflict," *Democracy, War, and Peace in the Middle East*, David Garnham and Mark Tessler, eds. (Bloomington, IN, c. 1995), 135.

Chapter 7

Liberalization, Democratization, and Stability in the Arab Middle East

I

There is a crying need for political liberalization and democratization in the Arab Middle East, for at least two important reasons. First and foremost, because under the complex conditions of the modern world, representative democracy is unquestionably the best—or the least imperfect—political system in existence, particularly if conjoined with a humane and caring economic system and social organization. Second, as we shall see in section II, liberalization and democratization in the Arab countries can serve to reduce if not end the Arab-Israeli conflict. If that is true, it would add to the discussion, in chapter 6, of Arab-Israeli economic relations and cooperation as a possible conflict-reducing factor.

As many writers on the subject have observed, little democratization and only very modest liberalization have unfortunately occurred so far in the Arab Middle East—in the Arab World as a whole. As Shukri B. Abed observes in "Democracy and the Arab World,"[1] "a quick look at the political map of the Arab world reveals that of the 21 Arab states, only one—Lebanon—boasts anything even approximating a Western-style democratic regime. And even this lone Arab country, with its Western-style parliamentary system, has been on the verge of collapse for years—precisely because of the inherently *nondemocratic* principle embodied in the Lebanese constitution: Maronite Christians were granted certain privileges over other major religious groups (the Druze, the Muslims, and even other Christian sects)."[2] What modest moves toward liberalization and democratization have taken place have been almost wholly confined to Jordan and Egypt.[3] For instance, Curtis R. Ryan [4] speaks of Jordan's "nascent stages of political liberalization" that closely followed the crisis of the Gulf War.[5] He notes, for example, that "Jordan's political landscape was transformed with the liberalization and democratization process, culminating in the lifting of martial law, the legalization of political parties, and elections of representatives to the lower house of Parliament. But the state maintained its coercive capabilities and above all the liberalization of the parliamentary level was the cooptive mechanism intended, in part, to maintain the legitimacy of the hereditary monarchy at the pinnacle of the Jordanian political system."[6]

A more complex situation exists in Egypt. Larbi Sadiki[7] maintains that "Egypt's democratic experiments are quintessential forms of political liberalisation as against democratisation." That is, Egypt's "democratic initiatives consist of controlled liberalisation, that is, liberalisation from the top that is designed to ease pressure from below engendered by acute socio-economic malaise."[8] There exists a "multiparty system as well as a relatively free press," which enable "opposition parties to express their views on political and social matters,. . . the institution of greater civil and political liberties, and procedural minimums (universal adult suffrage, elections, parties . . . .), power is still wielded unilaterally from the top down in virtually the same absolutist fashion by the same power cliques." Its "political liberalisations [therefore] qualify as classic cases of tutelary democracy or liberalised authoritarianism."[9] Again, "Egypt is unquestionably the Arab world's pace-setter. Egypt, however, does not always set the best example. This is at least true with regard to democratic stirrings." Egypt's "crossing of the democratic threshold" would be a "spill-over effect or, at least, a demonstration effect in the rest of the Arab world . . . [Its] present dicing with democracy has, however, thus far been fraught with tensions and contradictions."[10] Again,

> Party legalisation must be cleared by the semi-governmental Political Parties Committee (PPC). It keeps on rejecting the application for legalisation by the Muslim Brotherhood, potentially the most formidable opposition to the ruling NDP. Nor is it easy for secular parties to obtain legalisation. . . . A majority of PPC's board is made up of NDP members, including the Consultative Council president and the Ministers for the Interior and Justice.[11]

Sadiki sums up the situation in the Arab Middle East, with these words: "While notions of Western secularization and democratisation are based on respect for the rules and procedures of citizenship and on human rights, the opposite is more or less true of similar Arab processes. The attendant corollary is violence and counter-violence."[12]

II

Notwithstanding the formidable obstacles that the Palestine Authority will clearly encounter in 2000, when—on the best case scenario—it attempts to negotiate the creation of a Palestinian state, not only from the extreme Israeli right but also, quite possibly from the then-Israeli government—even though Labor won the elections in May 1999—if not also from Hamas and Islamic Jihad, let us imagine that a Palestinian state—or a Palestinian state federated with Jordan—already exists in the West Bank and the Gaza Strip in the year 2000, or, at the latest, during the first decade of the twenty-first century. Let us also imagine that, pursuant to a comprehensive settlement, Israel withdraws from the Golan and southern Lebanon, and Syrian troops simultaneously withdraw from Lebanon, leaving a stable, genuinely Lebanese government.

If all these formidable "ifs" are somehow realized, a root cause of actual and potential insurgency, terrorism, war, and other assorted forms of violence in the region would be eliminated. Even then, deeper causes of instability would continue to exert their baleful influence and jeopardize the prospects for a *lasting* peace in the region.

By the still deeper sources of instability I do not principally mean the seemingly endemic inter-Arab political, economic, territorial, and strategic divisions and rivalries, like those that precipitated the Gulf War; although the destabilizing influence of these divisions and rivalries is undeniable. Or rather, these tensions and divisions themselves are in considerable measure due to what I believe is the deepest source of actual and potential instability, and the greatest enemy of lasting peace in the region. I have in mind the absence of democracy in the Arab countries, briefly described in section I, and the slow, halting process of liberalization and democratization in certain of them. The role that the absence of democracy has, in my view, played in the creation and evolution of the Palestine Problem and the overall Arab-Israeli conflict, has already been touched upon in earlier chapters.

It is clear, I think, that the preceding remarks do not entail that the internecine problems and conflicts, together with their baleful consequences with respect to the Arab-Israeli conflict as a whole, including Arab terrorism, would *not* have arisen in this century had the Arab states been a model of political legitimacy and democracy. Similarly, it does not follow that the political problems pertaining to the future of Palestine would not have arisen had they, and the various British proposals designed to resolve them, been publicly debated and democratically decided; although it is not implausible to suppose that in that case the history of the Palestine Problem and the Arab-Israeli conflict would have been significantly different. At best, the absence of democracy in the Arab world can only account for *one* important thread in the tangled skein of the Arab-Israeli conflict. As we have seen, the conflict's precipitants and deep-lying causes, together with their violent outcomes, involve the contributions of a large number of major historical and cultural forces.

Quite apart from the role of the authoritarian political system in the Arab world in the rise and evolution of the Arab-Israeli conflict, it is necessary to address the question of whether liberalization and democratization, or continued liberalization and democratization in the Arab Middle East, *would tend* to create the requisite climate for the conflict's final peaceful resolution. Because of this question's importance for the central themes of the present book, the rest of this section will be devoted to it.

As stated at the end of the last chapter, Mark Tessler and Marilyn Gorbschmidt maintain the double thesis that "greater political liberalization and democracy in the Arab world may . . . reduce the likelihood of armed conflict between Arabs and Israelis [1], and it may also create a climate in which diplomatic efforts designed to address the underlying causes of the conflict will have a greater chance of success [2]."[13] These two central theses will now be critically examined.

To establish the first thesis [(1)], the authors attempt to show (a) that it is highly unlikely for disputes between democracies to lead to war; and (b) that democracy in the Arab world, if it does come, would very likely exemplify the same pattern. With regard to (2), they think that "there are at least two sets of reasons to believe that democratization in the Arab world would increase the prospects for a peaceful resolution of the Arab-Israeli dispute."[14]

I shall consider theses (1)(a) and (1)(b) in turn, then turn to thesis (2).

The authors provide convincing historical support for thesis (1)(a). They cite several studies that show that although democracies have been involved in numerous wars with nonliberal states, they have not fought other democracies.[15]

In response to the objection that the supposed relationship between democracy and peace does not really exist, that "societies with greater wealth have more to lose and are therefore reluctant to go to war,"[16] they point to studies that demonstrate "that peace among democracies cannot be explained by level or rate of development, by political stability, or by the lack of common borders."[17] They admit that although the Arab-Israeli conflict would take a very different direction if the Arab world became more democratic, they maintain that that would not *necessarily* make the Arab countries readier to negotiate and compromise. Nor, we might add, does thesis (1)(a) entail that in the absence of democracy or of democratization, the Arab states would *not* negotiate—or would be unlikely to negotiate—a peaceful settlement of the conflict.

Two sets of reasons are adduced by our authors for believing that democratization in the Arab world would increase the prospects for the conflict's peaceful resolution. The first is that "the processes and calculations shaping political decision-making in Arab states would be vastly different than they are at present,"[18] and so would diminish these states' belligerence toward Israel. The second is that "the attendant changes would have an important impact on Israeli perceptions and, more specifically, would reduce the security concerns that play such a significant role in the formation of Israeli foreign and defense policy."[19]

I think the second reason is correct. But the first reason is problematic with respect to those Arab states that are presently not at peace with Israel, e.g., Syria and Iraq,[20] given the deep, long-standing sources of hostility toward Israel in these countries. Again, our authors take it for granted that Israel is a *bona fide* democracy, which is far from evident, given the fact that both Israeli Arabs and a sizeable segment of its own Jewish population, Eastern Jews, have been relegated to second-class citizenship—quite apart from Israel's treatment of the Palestinian population in those parts of the West Bank and Gaza Strip it still occupies.

In sum, what is needed is specific and more direct evidence supporting the contention that "Arab democratization would increase the prospects for a peaceful resolution of the Arab-Israeli dispute" [(2)].[21] It is not enough to say that "to the extent that decision-making about war and peace is diffused, for example, subject to scrutiny by rival politicians and by a public that must ultimately bear the costs of military conflict, it is likely that Arab governments would resort to war only in the last resort and that at least some military confrontations would therefore be avoided."[22]

Finally, our authors note that if such issues as Palestinian statelessness are left unaddressed, "the conflict will fester no matter how democratic the Arab world might become."[23] That is certainly true.

In conclusion, although Tessler's and Grobschmidt's case for the connection between democracy and the absence of war in general appears to be well-established, their view that under the specified conditions that relation is likely to hold in the case of the Arab countries that are still technically at war with Israel, is more speculative, being essentially *a priori*. Indeed, unless the Golan is returned to Syria, I doubt that a future democratic regime in Syria would result in peace with Israel; just as I believe that, even under its present, authoritarian regime, the return of the Golan may in fact prompt Syria to make peace with Israel. Similarly in the case of Iraq, we can only speculate that democracy may lead to an end of Iraqi belligerence toward Israel—or, for that matter, toward any of its Arab neighbors.

It would certainly help in the present discussion if one could know what the majority of Arabs in the various Middle East Arab countries *presently* feel and think about the Palestine problem: in particular, whether they would be willing to see a recurrence of belligerence between their countries and Israel in another effort to "liberate" the whole of erstwhile Palestine, or even to create a Palestinian state in the West Bank and Gaza Strip; although I hazard the guess that, for rather obvious military, and, in some cases, political, reasons, the answer to both would be "no." We also do not know whether, at any future time, the Syrian people would be willing to go to war with Israel in order to liberate the Golan, although one can, I think, hazard the guess that the answer to that question too would be "no." Precisely because of the great restrictions on freedom of speech and the press in much of the Arab world, the fear of ordinary citizens to say what they think and feel about their rulers and governments, and the prevailing economic and political conditions in their own country, reliable answers to these questions are very hard to come by.

Tessler et al. stress that "the availability of legitimate channels for public debate and protest [in the Arab world] would most likely reduce the frequency and intensity of popular demonstrations over real and alleged foreign grievances, including those relating to the conflict with Israel."[24] Perhaps. But since the grievances relating to the conflict with Israel are as real as can be, the democratic channels for public debate and protest that would replace popular demonstrations may in fact favor a military rather than a negotiated solution to the conflict! In an important degree, the actual situation would depend, as I said, on how far non-Palestinian Arabs in the region—many of whom now belong to a generation with little or no personal knowledge of the Palestine Problem or of the series of wars from 1948 on—would be ready to make the necessary sacrifices for another military confrontation with Israel on behalf of the Palestinian cause. The same would apply to the Syrians' willingness to fight to recover the Golan.

In an attempt not to oversimplify the actual situation, our authors add that the "availability of legitimate channels for public debate and protest" would not decrease the ordinary Arab's sympathy to the Palestinian cause.

But they think that it is "probably of secondary importance to most Arab men and women"[25] —which I think is true, albeit not for the reasons they give. Rather, for the reasons I gave earlier, I believe that ordinary non-Palestinian Arabs have grown simply tired of the issue, particularly in the absence of, for example, the fiery rhetoric that used to issue forth from Arab leaders and the Arab media, and from the frequent public demonstrations and public marches. Nevertheless, I agree that "under conditions of greater democracy, it ["public protest and expressions of opposition" to Israel] would no longer be needed as a proxy for complaints that are in fact much higher on most people's agenda but which governments prevent from being the focus of serious political discourse."[26]

Even as things stand, i.e., in the effective absence of democracy in the Arab world, I believe that (with the notable exception of Saddam Hussein), Arab *leaders* lack the stomach for another war with Israel, knowing that it would be at least as disastrous as the past wars. That fact, coupled with the Soviet Union's disintegration and the end of its support to Syria and Iraq, as well as the Arabs' clear realization (exemplified most recently during the 1991 Gulf War) that the United States would not hesitate to come to Israel's aid whenever it is threatened, has given the Arab countries added reasons for caution and realism. These factors, I believe, constitute the greatest present deterrents to any Arab state's military encounter with Israel. They are also, I believe, the factors that have kept the peace between Syria and Israel since Israel's Lebanese campaigns.[27]

Finally, at the time of their writing, our authors believed that a change in the "political culture and political economy of key Arab states" may change the long-standing Israeli perception of such Arab states as Syria as intransigent, making it "more difficult for Israelis to argue, and in many cases believe, that peace with the Arab world is impossible and that any search for compromise and accommodation would be meaningless. In particular, Israeli hard-liners would find it more difficult to reject calls for an exchange of land for peace."[28] But since these words were written, Israeli hardliners have not found it difficult at all to reject Yitzhak Rabin's and Shimon Perez' "land for peace" policy, not only with regard to the Golan but also the West Bank and Gaza Strip.

III

If Tessler's and Gorbschmidt's claim about the relation between democratization in the Arab world and prospects for a negotiated settlement of the Arab-Israeli conflict is on the whole true, it would follow, other things being equal, that democratization would tend to bring increasing stability in, or increasingly reduce, the instability of the region. But in addition to its possible contribution to regional stability, democracy is unquestionably desirable in its own right, being arguably the best or least imperfect political system human beings have so far devised. If democracy does come about, it would be a blessing for the Arab Middle East, especially compared to the political, economic, and social systems under which they have suffered for millennia. For one thing, as David Beetham demonstrates in *The Legitimation of Power*,[29] liberal democracy (albeit always flawed in the real world) legitimates a country's political power and authority, and those who are at the helm of the state. The subordinates justify or legitimate the existing power structure and power relationship by virtue of the consonance of their beliefs and values with those of the dominants, and consequently, publicly express their consent to, hence their legitimation of, the dominants' authority.

This naturally leads to the crucial practical question of how the process of liberalization and democratization can be initiated or strengthened in traditionally authoritarian countries with no prior history of liberalism or popular democracy. When we consider the recent "derisory" record (Beetham) of democracy outside Western liberal capitalist democracies, the difficulty of that task becomes more evident. As Beetham writes, "there are very few countries in the less developed world which have been able to sustain a system of open party competition allied to freedoms of expression and association for any length of time."[30] Since the fall of Soviet communism, some Eastern European countries, and Russia above all, demonstrate with every passing day the struggle of liberal capitalism and of democracy to take root even in *developed* countries which had no historical experience of them, or like some other East European countries, are having to relearn the "habit" of democracy after decades of communist rule.

Beetham singles out two characteristics of *underdeveloped* countries that make it particularly difficult for them to attain liberal democracy. The first is the underdeveloped state of their economy, in part as a result of the state's playing a leading role in their economic development. Thus "the electoral system has to carry the strain of competition for scarce economic resources as well as the contest for political power (Clapham, 1985, ch. 3)."[31] We already touched in Section I on the central role the governments of the various Arab countries play in their economic system, although Saudi Arabia, the Gulf Emirates, and Libya currently do not, and, until some time in the twenty-first century will not, suffer from economic scarcity. That is, as long as their oil supplies last. The same will be true of Iraq when the present UN economic embargo is lifted.

Beetham's "second relevant feature of underdevelopment," namely "the sharp economic inequalities and dislocations that characterize the process of capitalist penetration of traditional economic relationships, and the early stages of industrialisation,"[32] is not, I believe, particularly relevant to the Arab countries, whether they have a quasi-capitalist or a socialist economic system: not that—for different reasons—they are free from gross inequalities between rich and poor!

Given Beetham's important first point, together with the implications he draws from his two points (on pages 172ff.), and the absence of a tradition of democracy, the prospects for progressive liberalization and democratization in the Arab world may seem to be dim indeed. In fact, outside of Lebanon, Jordan, Egypt, and Morocco, there is probably little understanding, among the general populace, of what democracy really is or involves. Even in the aforementioned countries the idea of "sovereignty of the people," including a multi-party system, appears to be largely a dream of relatively small groups of Western-educated and Westernized liberals in search of ways to turn the dream into reality.[33] Colonial rule is inherently authoritarian, undemocratic. It is not surprising therefore that during the British and French colonial period in the Middle East, the "natives" were not enabled to learn, or to learn properly, how to govern themselves, particularly how to establish a democratic political system, once they became independent. The British and French did create and rely on cadres of lower- and middle-level civil servants, but were careful to keep the top ranks and positions for themselves. Certainly that was the case in Palestine. Such training as the indigenous civil servants received simply did not equip them to function in positions of leadership in a democratic post-colonial state. Nor did the colonial powers teach the population as a whole what democracy is or means.

A separate treatise would be needed for a sufficiently probing study of the forces inimical to the democratization—or continued democratization—of the contemporary Arab Middle East, particularly for the working-out of a concrete, practical prescription for harnessing *existing* traditions and practices, attitudes, values, and beliefs favorable to the evolution of the Arab states into democracies. In the next, final section, I shall offer some modest, tentative suggestions along these lines, to round off the discussion in this chapter.

IV

Underlying my suggestions in this section is the basic assumption that if democracy is to become a reality in the Arab Middle East, the reformers must build on the existing indigenous values and traditions, attitudes, and societal institutions and practices. Democracy can only succeed and last if it grows organically from the culture and is not mechanically grafted upon it from outside as a mere imitation of Western representative democracy. In response to the question: "Do you believe democracy as it exists in the developed capitalist countries is possible in the Third World?" the writer Gabriel Garcia Marquez is reported to have said: "Democracy in the developed world is a product of their own development and not the other way round. To try to implant it in the raw state in countries (like those of Latin America) with quite different cultures is as mimetic and unrealistic as trying to implant the Soviet system there."[34]

Assuming for the sake of argument that the principle of popular sovereignty presently enjoys general acceptance among the Arab populations in the Middle East,[35] rather than gradually coming into acceptance during the coming years or decades, it is not unlikely that most Arab countries will first pass through a transitional stage, consisting in what Beetham calls a "mixed' constitutional order." That is, a political system in which the principle of popular sovereignty coexists with some other legitimating principle; e.g., the principle of traditionalism and heredity, "underpinning a range of powers accorded the monarch [or other ruler], from largely ceremonial ones . . . to a much more executive role . . . [or] a theocratic principle of political appointment, and the belief in a divine rather than merely human source of law."[36] Only later would countries with a "mixed" system evolve, *if they do*, into what Beetham calls "a pure expression of the principle of popular sovereignty."[37]

I said above that "most Arab countries will probably first pass through a transitional stage." As Beetham observes, Jordan and Morocco at present exemplify one sort of "mixed" political system, while among non-Arab countries in the region, the Islamic republic of Iran exemplifies a different form of "mixed" political system. On October 5, 1992, under pressure from the United States and its own political activists, Kuwait took a very short first step toward a "mixed" political system, by holding eagerly awaited elections. It was a very modest step indeed, since only men—and only those whose families had resided in Kuwait prior to 1925—were eligible to vote. Significantly, the majority of voters came from the opposition, which had been long seeking political change. But given the al-Sabah family's tight hold on the country, that first liberalizing move was not followed by the gradual empowerment of the Kuwaiti people as a whole.[38]

To bring about increasing liberalization and democratization, progressive elements in the Arab World need to harness existing societal forms and structures to that end. At first it may be necessary for them to focus on those countries that show special promise and can become models for the other Arab countries to emulate. Unfortunately, Lebanon has all but lost, at least for the time being, whatever opportunities it had in these regards. Unfortunately, the 15-year cataclysm it suffered provides a ready—albeit invalid—argument to the politically conservative or reactionary governments of some Arab states, against liberalization or democratization.[39]

In his interview with Marquez referred to earlier, the interviewer responded to the writer's answer by asking: "So you think democracy is a kind of luxury for rich countries?" Marquez replied: "Remember that democracy carries with it the defence of human rights,"[40] adding: "I'm not talking about democratic principles but democratic forms."[41] With regard to the Arab Middle East the issue before us is about democratic principles-cum-democratic forms: about democratic institutions and practices as concrete embodiments of democratic principles *and* forms. In the absence of either, democracy cannot exist.

The following are the main indigenous forces that, in principle, i.e., if properly utilized, would, I believe, favor democracy in the Arab world. The first is the fundamentally "Bedouin Mind"—the Bedouin traditions, loyalties, and values, including their scheme of individual and communal virtues and vices which, I believe, continue to inform the Arab mind in obvious and in subtle ways. These formative influences go back several millennia, to the early history of the Arabian peninsula, perhaps even to pre-Islamic times. They still run deep underneath the surface of the, in many respects, superficially modernized, Westernized strata of much urban Arab society. Or to change the metaphor, they constitute the deep springs of action of the generality of people in the culture, and are particularly efficacious because of their largely unconscious character.[42]

One important form that influence takes is in the largely communitarian character of Middle Eastern rural and urban Arab society, which appears to derive historically from the nomadic Bedouin communitarian form of life. As a full-fledged form of societal life, it embodies and defines Arab society's traditions and values, economic, political and social forms, and the plethora of human relationships. Indeed, in so far as Arab society continues to be informed or influenced by communitarian ideals, including what is now called the "ethic of care or caring,"[43] it continues to be largely other-directed, socially concerned, responsibility-driven, significantly more cooperative than competitive, and, consequently, favorable to social and political justice and democracy. Even in the large metropolitan centers, strong personal and community values and ties survive, although more uneasily than in the villages and small towns.[44]

Islam, including present-day Islamic fundamentalism, is another force of great significance for our discussion. Because of its special importance, I shall consider it separately a little later. At the moment I shall concentrate on the other factors I listed.

I said that, theoretically speaking, Bedouin societal and cultural forces are favorable to liberalization and democratization. The question is how or why they are so, and how they need to be drawn upon to help bring about the desired outcome. My answer, very briefly, is the following:

As in the case of other traditional societies, the strong, essentially Bedouin Arab sense of loyalty is fundamentally personal, particular, clannish. In the political and military spheres, it is loyalty to a particular political or military (often military-cum-political) leader, the head or most prominent member of the power elite, such as the Emir or the King.[45] Hence *if* the sense of loyalty and the moral responsibilities and obligations that attach to it can be somehow broadened, hence transferred to and transformed into loyalty to the particular country or people as a whole and its welfare, an important step would have been taken toward the creation of a sense of national or of popular identity and unity: a necessary first step itself toward a people's empowerment, "people power."[46] The "tribal" loyalties or "personality cult," endemic to the Arab world and a main source of its factionalism, divisiveness, and instability, would then gradually disappear. An important condition for the rise of the concept of "the people" as the repository of political sovereignty would then be satisfied. Again, in countries such as Lebanon where a strong, clear sense of national identity is still absent, and where people only identify with their immediate communities, the existence of economic, political, social, or other important concerns they share with the members of other communities in the country should ultimately bring the entire country together in that sense of oneness or unity which the concept of popular sovereignty presupposes.

In discussing the principle of popular sovereignty in his book, Beetham makes two main points that underline the significance of the preceding considerations for the question of liberalization and democratization in the Arab world. His first point is that "once it is accepted that the source of political authority resides in the people, it becomes important to know who exactly constitutes 'the people.'"[47] This is true because, as I have indicated, the concept of popular sovereignty logically presupposes the concept of "the people." A national group must have the latter concept on which to ground the idea of its sovereignty as "a people."

Beetham's second point is that "the importance of the idea of popular sovereignty . . . [in the context of his discussion of the change from the hereditary principle of the *ancien regimes* to the principle that "the state belonged . . . to the people"] was that it gave the cultural, ethnic and historical communities with which people could identity, and around which they could be mobilised, a political salience they had not previously enjoyed."[48]

Middle Eastern ethic/morality of honor, dishonor, and shame, mentioned earlier in a note, is intimately connected with Arab society's communitarian character, in which the community radiates in roughly concentric circles from the family—particularly the extended family—as the center, through the complex kinship-relationships of the clan, to close and not-so-close friends, to acquaintances, and, finally, to strangers. A man's or a woman's honor is more, considerably more, than personal or even family honor, and tends to radiate to and touch the honor of the entire community in which the members are integral parts.

I cannot attempt to show this here; but a morality of justice and of human rights—"morality in the narrow sense" as it is sometimes called—can successfully coexist with a reformed and *transformed,* hence egalitarian, morality of honor, dishonor, and shame, freed from its patriarchal, male-dominated character that has relegated women to a glaringly subordinate and inferior status to men for thousands of years.

Although a hotly debated issue among feminist moral philosophers and others,[49] the same can be shown to be true of the Middle Eastern virtue-ethic of "caring and responsibility" *vis-à-vis* the dominant Western "justice/rights" ethic. In fact, the concept of equal human rights now appears to enjoy wide acceptance in the Arab world, especially among educated men and women, and constitutes a major foundation-stone on which democratic societal structures can be raised. But only the future can tell to what extent that concept has begun to weaken the culture's hierarchic patriarchal character by, among other things, weakening the male-sexist aspects of the honor/dishonor morality without necessarily destroying what is valuable in it, such as the values on which the morality rests and the worthwhile modes of behavior it enjoins.

I now turn to the possible role of Islam, particularly the role of Islamic fundamentalism, in relation to our discussion.

According to the editor of an influential Muslim fundamentalist Cairo newspaper who appeared on a recent American television program on Islamic fundamentalism,[50] Islam is "identical with" democracy. He therefore argued that a Muslim fundamentalist government in Egypt—and presumably, in other Islamic countries—would be genuinely democratic. Now it is true that the ideals of Islam are ideals of equality and social justice: ideals also fundamental to democracy. And since Islam, together with Arab nationalism, is a powerful and pervasive force in the Arab world, it may seem to follow that a genuinely Islamic political system would make the realization of these values in the society as a whole a prime political objective. But as Beetham argues, a secular state is a *sine qua non* of a democratic political system. Where church and state are not separate, only a "mixed" political system, such as the one in Iran or in Saudi Arabia, would be possible. Moreover, like any other kind of "mixed" system, a theocratic "mixed" system is heir to all the internal tensions and conflicts endemic to a dual, hence divided, source of authority and power. Stated otherwise, a genuinely pluralistic society is hard to envisage when those who are at the helm of the ship of state believe that they possess the "absolute" or "ultimate" truth.

Again, although Islam is a great unifying spiritual force in the Arab and Muslim worlds, the resurgence of Shiite and Sunni fundamentalism has led to serious ideological and political divisions; e.g., in Egypt, Algeria, Jordan, Lebanon, the West Bank, and Gaza Strip.

The question therefore remains whether an Islamic state can provide a base or matrix for the region's gradual democratization. For one of my earlier suppositions was that, at least theoretically speaking, a "mixed" theocratic political system can serve as a transitional stage to a "pure" democracy. In order to answer the question, I shall follow Beetham's distinction between three different conceptions of "Islamic state." Beetham writes: "At a minimum it ["Islamic state"] can mean a state which gives protection to the institutions and practice of the Islamic faith."[51] In this minimal sense an Islamic state of the "mixed" variety can clearly serve in the desired capacity. The state's allegiance to Islam in the way described would not prevent it from being a "secular" state, or from having a multi-party political system that includes a viable political party inspired by the moral ideals of Islam. Beetham continues: "More substantially, it can mean a state whose policies are themselves conducive to Muslims living a life in accordance with the requirements of their religion."[52] That (presumably "mixed") sort of Islamic state too is not necessarily inimical or unresponsive to democratization, and certainly may in time lead to a democratic-

Islamic state in the minimal sense. Third, "[a] more stringent demand is that the state should embody the *shari'a*, or Islamic law, in its own legislation and judicial procedures; though, here again, what this amounts to in practice will depend on how narrowly the *shari'a* itself is to be interpreted."[53] Theoretically, this type of Islamic state too is not incompatible with a representative form of government, even though it grants a pre-eminent status to religion and does not separate church and state. I therefore concur with Beetham's view that, with the exception of the fourth and most stringent sense of 'Islamic state,' i.e., a state in which the state is subordinated to the "religious project of creating a spiritually transformed community, inspired by 'the true Islamic mentality and moral attitudes,'"[54] "the ideal of an Islamic state or Islamic order is compatible with and can be realised within, any constitutional form: monarchical, representative, or whatever. This is because its primary concern is to specify the purposes or goals that the state should serve, rather than the source from which its political authority is to be derived."[55]

Various Middle East scholars, including Tessler and Gorbschmidt, emphasize the reformist character of current Islamist movements, and see the support they have been receiving as the result of the "absence of democracy and the existence of unresolved domestic economic problems." That, they claim, is a basis for "popular discontent and demands for accountable government."[56] At the same time they follow certain other Middle East scholars in holding that "ideologically, the reasoning of religious groups and their socio-political programs are too political to appeal to traditional mainstream Muslims."[57] Some scholars also correctly caution against assumptions about the "monolithic nature of Islam and Islamic 'fundamentalism' and [warn us] to recognize the diversity of ideological interpretations and the even greater diversity of actual practice in Muslim societies."[58]

Because of the crucial roles the West, particularly the United States, already plays in the region, we finally need to ask what role the West can play in advancing the causes of liberalization and democratization, to the extent that they exist in the Arab world, helping reform to continue and perhaps accelerate. My answer, very briefly, is that whatever economic, political, and cultural influence the West can exert in that direction, is best attempted in ways other than by directly tying official economic and technical assistance to the Arab states to democratic reform. As far as I can tell, such official pressure, if any,[59] has had no visible effect on their political systems, and is bound to continue to fall on fallow ground. In fact, any Western attempt to exert direct pressure of that sort on Arab countries is bound to intensify the strong anti-Western—especially anti-American—sentiments of many ordinary Arabs: above all, the growing anti-Western sentiments of the Islamic fundamentalists, who reject out of hand Western ("Crusader") culture and values, including, at least in some instances, liberal, Western-style democracy. Their rejection of any sort of accommodation with Israel is part and parcel of their hostility to the West. Moreover, the West's interest in the Middle East's economic and political reform, if any, is bound to decline significantly in the 21st century, as the region's oil reserves are depleted—and with it, the region's economic and strategic importance for the West.

Private Western concerns, and the economic, scientific, and technical assistance they provide to the region too are not particularly well-equipped to stimulate the process of liberalization and democratization. Given their primarily profit-making concerns and preoccupations, Western companies and corporations are even less equipped than their government agencies to stimulate such reforms.

The West can best help to bring about economic and social as well as political liberalization and reform in the region by "indirection." I mean through its influence on the attitudes and minds, hence on the behavior, of Western-educated Middle Eastern intellectuals and professionals. The problem, of course, is the continuing "brain drain" of young Western-educated or westernized Middle Easterners; since only those who stay in the region or return to it after receiving their education or training in the West can be really effective in helping to bring about the desired reforms. Even then the potential for change that they represent may not be realized. Their social environment may force them to conform to the status quo and give up their "newfangled" ideas for the sake of being accepted by their families, relatives, and community, hence to survive and to function in the culture. Or they themselves may put aside as useless or impracticable in the authoritarian, largely traditional Arab culture, the liberal, democratic ideas and values to which they had been exposed. Or thirdly, they may abandon these ideas and values out of fear of ostracism and even bodily harm as "stooges of the West," at the hands of anti-Western elements. Yet it is only such enlightened intellectuals and professionals in the thick of the region's economic, educational, scientific, social, or political life who may be best-positioned to inculcate and spread the ideals of sexual equality and equal human rights, representative democracy, and the freedoms and civil liberties that are the *sine qua non* of an enlightened and moral personal and social existence.

V

If, as was argued in Section II, liberalization and democratization, and, above all, full-fledged democracy, can be instrumental in reducing the regime of conflict between Arabs and Israel, that fact would argue in favor of consistent and sustained efforts in the Arab world, both by the rulers and the ruled, to bring about these salutary changes, quite apart from their value in furthering the general welfare and happiness. However, some Arab or Muslim scholars and intellectuals argue that "Western-style democracy" is unsuited for the Arab (and Muslim) world; that what it needs is an Islamist state, based on the moral-religious, social, economic, and political-legal dictates of Islam. Indeed, the conflict-reducing potential of democracy, or of liberalization and democratization, would hardly impress the militant Islamists, since they oppose any reduction in the Arabs' armed struggle against Israel.

According to Shukri B. Abed, (1) some Arab intellectuals maintain that the Arab countries' social and political malaise is not due to the absence of democracy: rather, the absence of democracy is "only a result, a reflection of these miseries. In the eyes of such thinkers, democracy is a natural development of changing socioeconomic conditions and therefore not something that can be arbitrarily imposed on any given society. Such conditions of prosperity, literacy, a well-developed middle class, and an enlightened leadership are . . . necessary and perhaps sufficient conditions for the emergence of democratic forms of government."[60] (2) The more radical, pro-Islam view all too frequently "translates into an implacable stance that dismisses democracy along with all things Western. . . . Democracy, [as] an imported idea. . . has no room in Islam and . . . its supporters, 'those who were schooled in Western Civilization, should be fought against.' "[61] But (3) "according to many defenders of the 'Islamic solution,' Islam is in and of itself liberal and democratic, therefore compatible with the ideas of the modern world."[62] "It is hardly fair, then, to portray Islam as inherently antidemocratic and the single greatest obstacle to political progress in the Arab world, especially when awareness and suspicion of democracy and other Western exports is shared by many staunchly opposed to the Islamic movements."[63]

Since Section II dealt with claim (3) to some extent, I shall concentrate on claims (1) and (2). With regard to claim (3) it need only be added that any "democratic" Islamic state would be necessarily quite *different* from any of the present Arab and non-Arab Islamic states, such as Saudi Arabia and the other Gulf States, Egypt, Libya, Afghanistan, Malaysia, or Indonesia.

Unlike claim (2), claim (1) is in agreement with the present author's view in that democracy, a highly desirable political system in general, not just for the West but also for the Arab and other Muslim countries. It differs from that view in asserting that the Arab countries are not ready for democracy—a view I recall some of my Syrian students at the American University of Beirut defended in the 1950s or 1960s. These students correctly argued that a literate and politically educated electorate was necessary for democracy, and that, at that time, such an electorate was lacking in the Arab world. But they incorrectly concluded that what the Arab world needed were benevolent strongmen who would create an educational system that would school their people in democracy. It goes without saying that a mythical creature of that description has not subsequently turned up, and that democracy will scarcely see the light of day in the Arab world if, instead of relying on themselves to create—against all odds—the necessary changes in educational and social conditions, attitudes, behavior, and values, the people rely on their rulers to create democracy from above. As the reader will recall, Section II outlined what I believe are some of the required changes. Again, it is an error to think that democracy is an all-or-nothing state of affairs: that democracy is an all-or-nothing political system, and so can only come into existence fully formed, like Athena springing fully armed from Zeus' head; that it cannot evolve gradually over time. Certainly the citizens of *some* Arab countries, e.g., Lebanon, Jordan, and Egypt, if not also Syria, as well as the majority of Palestinians, are now as ready for democracy, with regard to political education and social conditions, as any time in the foreseeable future. Deferring democratization, or further democratization, in the hope that time will somehow bring it about, is simply wishful thinking. Since there can be degrees in which a political system is or is not democratic—albeit certain core features are requisite for a particular system's qualifying as a "minimal" or "essential" democracy [64] —so long as these core features are brought into existence in the Arab countries, their political system would be minimally democratic. In time the system could be enriched with additional democratic features, and its core features enhanced.

Again, the claim that the absence of democracy in the Arab world is a reflection or result of economic and social malaise, inverts the correct causal order, particularly if we remember that a nonauthoritarian, nonrepressive economic system designed to serve the general welfare, not powerful special interests; hence a system that respects the wage earner's human rights is the economic counterpart of a democratic political system.[65]

(2) The aforementioned second claim, which is part of a general anti-Western ideology or bias, is quite false, although not difficult to understand in a region that has long suffered under Western colonial rule. Its major premise, (a) that everything Western is bad for Arabs and Muslims, is false. Further, and more importantly for our purposes, (b) it commits a non sequitur in identifying democracy in general with what it prejudicially calls "Western-stye" democracy, and so, concluding (c) that democracy (in general) should be rejected. The claim's error stems from its ignoring the fact that as a type of political system democracy is not and cannot be the exclusive "domain" or "monopoly" of any particular culture, country, or society, Western or other; although, it is commonplace that in its modern, representative form, it first arose in the West. The fundamental question is not whether democracy should or should not be rejected because it is—or rather, was—a "Western" political system, but whether it—i.e., "government of the people, for the people, by the people"—is a *good* system. If it is, it simply makes no sense to reject it.

To sum up. The absence of democracy and the modest economic and political liberalization in the Middle East Arab countries formed the backdrop to the main subject of the chapter: the evaluation of Tessler's and Grobschmidt's claim that political liberalization and democratization in the Arab world may reduce the regime of war between Arabs and Israelis and help bring about diplomatic efforts to address the conflict's underlying causes. A critical examination of that claim showed that the authors' case for (a) the connection between democracy and the absence of war in general was well-established, their claim that (b) under the specified conditions that relation is likely to hold in the case of the Arab countries that are still at war with Israel, is more speculative. However, an important corollary of (b) is that, other things being equal, democratization would tend to make the Middle East politically more stable or less unstable: a corollary independently supported by Beetham's demonstration that democracy legitimates a state's political power and authority. That, together with the fact that democracy is the political system most conducive to the individual's fullest development and actualization, and to the attainment of the general welfare, strongly argued for its desirability in the Arab world as a whole.

The question of how democracy can best be established in the Middle East Arab countries, given the absence of a historical liberal political tradition, was next considered, and some modest and tentative ideas as to how it may grow or be helped to grow from the traditional culture, were presented. The discussion included an exploration of the possible role of the still-prevalent ethic/morality of honor, dishonor, and shame in relation to democracy, and the forms of Islamic state, if any, that are compatible with democracy.

Notes

1. *Democracy, Peace, and the Israeli-Palestinian Conflict*, Edy Kaufman, Shukri B. Abed, and Robert L. Rothstein, eds. (Boulder, CO, 1993), 189–211.

2. Ibid., 189. Italics in original.

3. Apart from the nondemocratic principle in its constitution, Lebanon before the 1975–1990 civil war was a "façade democracy." It had, as Abed notes, the machinery of a Western-style parliamentary system but lacked a proper understanding or appreciation of the values essential for a democracy proper, such as respect for the equal human and civil rights of all its citizens, and the use of the ballot as a means of effective representation and participation in the political process. In fact, Lebanon was (and continues to be) essentially a quilt of feudal fiefdoms.

4. "Jordan in the Middle East Peace Process: From War to Peace with Israel," *The Middle East Peace Process, Interdisciplinary Perspectives*, Ilan Peleg, ed. (Albany, NY, 1998), pp. 161–178.

5. Ibid., 168.

6. Ibid., 175. And, "almost two years ago [in 1991], the pragmatic king of Jordan allowed Muslim and leftist forces to run for election in the Jordanian Parliament. The Muslim forces and their supporters won about thirty-five out of eighty seats in the elections. Several women also ran for election, although none successfully. Incidentally, this was the first time in twenty-six years that elections were held in Jordan" (Shukri B.Abed, op cit., 190).

7. "The Impasse of Liberalising Arab Authoritarianism: The Cases of Algeria and Egypt," *Remaking the Middle East*, Paul J. White and William S. Logan, eds. (Oxford. New York, 1997), 59–85.

8. Ibid., 60.

9. Ibid.

10. Ibid., 65–66.

11. Ibid., 74.

12. Ibid., 78.

13. "Democracy in the Arab World and the Arab-Israeli Conflict," *Democracy, War, and Peace in the Middle East*, David Garnham and Mark Tessler, eds. (Bloomington, c 1995), 136.

14. Ibid., 143.

15. Op cit., 140–141.

16 Ibid., 141.

17 Ibid. For further discussion and support of that claim, see ibid., 141–143; including what the authors consider to be the kinds of structural constraints democracies have in place against war with other democracies. These constraints, they note, are absent "when the citizens of a democracy evaluate the behavior of nondemocratic states" (ibid., 143).

18 Ibid., 143.

19 Ibid.

20 But even in the latter case, as I stated earlier in a note, it is not impossible that democracy would help lead to peace between it and Israel.

21 Ibid., 146.

22 Ibid., 144.

23 Ibid., 145.

24 Ibid., 145–146.

25 Ibid.

26 Ibid., 146.

27 For Tessler's and Gorbschmidt's reply to the counter-theses of some analysts, viz. "that conclusions drawn from international relations literature on democracy, war, and peace are not applicable to the present-day Middle East," see ibid., 148–164.

28 Ibid., 146.

29 New Jersey, 1991.

30 Ibid., 171.

31 Ibid., 172.

32 Ibid. But note the implications Beetham draws on 172ff. in relation to his discussion of the difficulty of an underdeveloped country's attaining legitimacy.

33 The imperviousness of Saudi Arabia's and the Gulf Emirates' ruling elites to American and other Western progressive ideas, during and since the 1991 Gulf War, is a good example of the kind of powerful forces working against liberalization and democratization in the Arab world. Regarding Kuwait's post-Gulf War elections, see later.

34 Plinio Apuleyo Mendoza and Gabriel Garcia Marquez, *The Fragrance of Guava*, Ann Wright, tr. (London, 1983), 101.

35 Beetham believes that the idea of popular sovereignty is now universally accepted.

36 Ibid.

37 Ibid., 129, and *passim*.

38 From the time of its independence from France until the start of the civil war, Lebanon enjoyed the external machinery of representative government but lacked genuine popular sovereignty. In other words, it was a so-called facade democracy. It is hoped that in time Lebanon will genuinely realize what has been only formally and procedurally realized.

39 Can we realistically imagine that if the Arab-Israeli conflict is resolved in the coming years, liberal forces in the Arab countries will look to an Israel cleansed of the occupier's taint as a model to follow? It is an intriguing question.

40 Ibid., 102.

41 Ibid.

42 Cf. the following statements, by Monroe Berger, in *The Arab World Today* (Garden City, NY, 1964), 42 and 44, respectively: "Desert, village and city are intimately related to each other in Arab society. Many Islamic and purely Arab values derive from the desert." And, "though they constitute only a small and declining proportion of the Arab population, the bedouins are important for their role in creating the values of Arab civilization" (ibid., 43). Again: "Bedouin values still persist in Arab society through their early influence upon Islam and upon tribal loyalties."

43 For a sketch of that ethic, see my *Community and Communitarianism* (New York, 1999), especially Part II.

44 Intertwined with the ethic of caring and the majority's Islamic values and norms (or in the case of the Christian minorities, Christian values and norms), one finds the pervasive "Mediterranean" ethic and morality of honor, dishonor, and shame. But that ethic and morality are conspicuously sexist and hierarchical, in sharp contrast to the ethic of caring. The process of liberalization should therefore include sustained attempts to eliminate these sexist and hierarchic elements but endeavor to retain as much as possible what is of value in that scheme of virtues and vices.

45 The same tends to be true in the religious sphere, where allegiance is paid to a particular spiritual leader or to the most prominent religious leaders.

46 Something Lebanon seriously lacked and which, together with other disruptive forces—sectarianism and glaring economic disparities—helped bring about the recent internecine conflict.

47 Op. cit., 132.

48 Ibid.

49 See, for example, *Woman and Moral Theory*, Eva Feder Kittay and Diana T. Meyers, eds. (New York, 1987). See also *Community and Communitarianism*.

50 In an interview titled "Islamic Fundamentalism," aired on American Public Television.

51 Op. cit., 192.

52 Ibid.

53 Ibid.

54 Ibid.

55 Ibid., 192-193. Also note the following: "It is . . . critical, as [John L.] Esposito and [James F.] Piscatori note, to avoid assumptions about the monolithic nature of Islam and Islamic "fundamentalism" and to recognize "the diversity of ideological interpretations and the even greater diversity of actual practice in Muslim societies (1991, p. 440)." (Tessler et al., op cit., 29.) The authors' reference is to Esposito's and Piscatori's "Democratization and Islam," *The Middle East Journal*, vol. 43 (Summer 1991), 440. But also note that the Egyptian and Palestinian Hamas fundamentalists appear to envisage an Islamic state of the *fourth* type.

56 Op cit., 22. Cf. Jamal Sanad's following statement in his contribution to op cit.: "As long as governments in the Arab world resist political participation and the tolerance of different political opinions, the strength of Islam as a political ideology will continue to be a serious alternative." 13. (Quoted from Tessler et al., ibid., 22.) Note that Sanad is speaking of Islam as an alternative to popular political participation.

57 Quoted from Tessler et al., op cit., 23.

58 "Democratization and Islam," *The Middle East Journal*, vol. 45 (Summer 1991), 440.

59 I say "if any," since it is not self-evident that Western governments really want to see liberal democracy triumph in the Arab world. Beetham raises that question in a general way, in relation to the Third World as a whole, as follows: "If it could be shown that the economic development of the advanced capitalist societies was systematically connected to the underdevelopment of the colonial and post-colonial societies of the Third World, then we should have to conclude . . . that the security of liberal democracy in the former was dependent upon the conditions making for its insecurity in the latter. In other words, it would be doubtful whether the successful legitimacy of capitalist democracy could ever be other than a localised, not a universal one" (op cit., 178).

60 Shukri B. Abed, op. cit., 194.

61 Ibid., 195. The passage Abed quotes is by 'Ali M. Jraisheh and Muhammad Sharif al-Zaibaq, *The Methods of Cultural Invasion of the Islamic World* (Cairo, 1978); quoted in Tibi's lecture in Azumat, 87. Abed notes: "Tibi comments on this position as follows: 'Thus the fight against cultural invasion becomes the fight against democracy and its supporters, and the struggle for Islam turns into a struggle against democracy'" (ibid., 209).

62 Ibid., 195.

63 Ibid.

64 Including a free opposition party or free opposition parties; an appreciable degree of freedom of expression and of the press; religious freedom; a modicum of respect for human rights; and a legal system in which the powerful, including those who govern, are not above the law. (See also note 66.)

65 In a revealing program on public television on December 30, 1998, titled "Globalization and Human Rights," the consensus was that respect for individual human rights rather than sole concern with the "bottom line," is essential to ending the exploitation of workers by powerful companies and corporations and raising their standard of living. But respect for human rights is also of the essence of a democratic political system.

Chapter 8

Conclusion

"With a nod to its biblical character, Israel marked 50 years of modern statehood Thursday by celebrating its strength and vowing an eternal hold on Jerusalem.

Quoting from Hatikvah, which means "the hope," Netanyahu said 'hope gave us the immense strength we needed to rise from the ashes and start again. We overcame obstacles that no other nation has experienced.'

In the official ceremony, . . . there was no mention of the peace process or the conflict with Palestinians that still vexes the region until the last speech, by Ezer Weizman, the . . . president of Israel.

Weizman called for concluding peace with the Palestinians and said 'the sooner we reach this the better.' He also brushed aside platitudes to remind Israel that it still faces problems of unemployment, discrimination against Arab citizens and a burdensome occupation of southern Lebanon."[1]

After 50 years of statehood, and after winning the war, Israel is now closer than any time since its creation to winning the peace. But the long occupation of the West Bank and Gaza Strip, and East Jerusalem, is another matter, even if compared with the residual state of war that technically exists between it and Syria and Lebanon. Like a bad dream, its continued occupation of East Jerusalem and the greater part of the West Bank continues to haunt it with the prospect of seemingly unending unrest, instability, and Palestinian-Israeli conflict. Consequently, its brilliant military victories over the Arab states are bound to remain very incomplete victories so long as it clings to the land that Palestinians rightfully call their own. Only when the heavy chains binding occupier and occupied are broken, and Palestinians become their own masters, can real peace and stability in the region become more than a wistful hope. For then not just *sulh* but *salaam* should become the order of the day between the majority of West Bank and Gaza Palestinians, and Israel. Indeed, it is the fervent hope of all peace-loving persons that the Palestinian Islamists, including Hamas and Palestinian Islamic Jihad, would then accede to long-term *sulh* with Israel. Surely Israel's agreement to Palestinian independence should be proof positive of Israel's "veering toward peace."[2]

I spoke advisedly of Israel's "agreeing" to Palestinian independence. This is absolutely essential. It is essential that Palestinian independence should come about, not unilaterally as Yasser Arafat has declared or threatened more than once, but bilaterally, as part of the final settlement negotiations. In these negotiations, all the burning issues not dealt with in the transitional stage should be resolved through mutual consent and a spirit of genuine partnership, as befits neighbors who will coexist for all time. As Netanyahu had warned, a unilateral declaration of independence would almost certainly result in swift Israeli annexation of the West Bank and Gaza Strip, and the destruction of everything Palestinians and Israelis have worked to build, after decades of blood, sweat, and tears through the slow and painful peace process. The salutary change in the political climate with Ehud Barak's victory in the 1999 elections, Arafat has fortunately deferred his declaration of Palestinian statehood. Barak's and Arafat's latest meetings have centered on the Wye Agreement: with Barak trying to persuade Arafat "to agree to a slowdown" in its implementation; fearing that the withdrawal timetable contained in the agreement will make the 15 Israeli settlements in the West Bank vulnerable to Palestinian attack. "Any such violence would make it politically impossible for him to make compromises necessary for agreement on . . . such [issues] as the borders of whatever Palestinian nation might be established in the West Bank."[3]

In clinging to the West Bank, Gaza Strip, and East Jerusalem for so long, in the face of unremitting Palestinian and other Arab resistance, UN Security Resolutions, and recent U.S. pressure, Israel has sowed the wind and (since 1967) reaped the whirlwind, in "Samaria" and "Judea." It is particularly difficult to understand how, at least until the *Intifada*—and in spite of unremitting civil disobedience, freedom fighting, terrorism directed against it, both before and after that uprising—the Israeli government and people apparently continued to believe that the Palestinian masses would indefinitely accept—or resign themselves to—Israeli military subjection.

As in the case of the "road not taken" between 1948 and 1952, described in the *The Road Not Taken, Early Arab-Israeli Relations*[4] and referred to earlier in this book, when "a permanent peace [between Israel on the one hand and Transjordan, Syria, and Egypt on the other hand] came within reach, only to slip away for years to come,"[5] the region and the world missed another golden opportunity for peace in 1978, when Israel signed the Camp David Accords, and still another in 1979, when Israel and Egypt signed a peace treaty. In the last instance, despite Menachem Begin's agreement on a "Framework for Peace in the Middle East [,] . . . [which] set forth general principles and some specifics to govern a comprehensive peace settlement, focusing on the future of the West Bank and the Gaza Strip,"[6] Israel failed to carry the Framework agreement through. Instead, adamant that "Judea and Samaria" had to remain an inseparable part of modern Israel, Begin initiated the "facts on the ground" policy by allowing the creation of Jewish settlements in the West Bank and Gaza Strip: a policy that was religiously adhered to by his Likud successors; in particular, Yitzhak Shamir and Benjamin Netanyahu. Although that policy helped satisfy the aspirations of the settlers, the policy has not been a blessing to the Israeli people as a whole, or, even, to the Israeli policymakers. It has been inimical to Palestinian aspirations, a bone of contention between Palestinians and Israelis, and has been responsible for greatly exacerbating tensions and hostilities between them.[7] Above all, it has created a difficult problem concerning the territory and boundaries of a future Palestinian state. It is unfortunate that, when Israel signed the peace treaty with Egypt, its strongest adversary, Prime Minister Begin, did not seize the opportunity to resolve the Palestinian Problem but saw it as conveniently relieving pressure on his government to deal with that Problem. Instead, Israel thought of the Palestine Problem's resolution wholly in terms of its pet "Jordanian option," which it single-mindedly pursued at least until King Hussein, in 1988, renounced in favor of the Palestinians, Jordan's claims to the West Bank and East Jerusalem.[8] Had Israel's security and territorial concerns, among others, made it willing to resolve the Palestinian Problem in the way proposed in this book, in line with the wishes of the majority of Palestinians, the region would have been especially spared the 1982 Israeli invasion of Lebanon, and its aftermath—with, among other things, the invasion's heavy cost to the PLO, the innocent Palestinian men, women, and children in the Sabra and Shatila refugee camps who were mercilessly slaughtered by the Christian phalangists with Ariel Sharon's help, and the moral and psychological as well as human cost to Israel itself. Above all, its human and material cost to the Lebanese, whose capital was left in shambles as a result of the fighting between the Israeli forces and the PLO. It is an open question whether Israel would have also been spared the loss of life and limb that it has suffered in northern Israel and in the south Lebanon "security zone" had it granted statehood to the Palestinians prior to 1982, given the fact that Hezbollah guerrillas were already attacking northern Israel before the Lebanese invasion, and the security zone's creation. But I think it most unlikely that Israel would have thought it necessary to invade Lebanon—let alone reach the outskirts of Beirut—merely to try to eliminate Hezbollah. One would think that Israel would have been more interested in seeking a resolution of the Golan issue with Syria. In any event, once Palestinian statehood becomes a reality, I think that Syria would be strongly inclined to seek a resolution of the Golan issue, perhaps to the extent of compromising on its longstanding demand for a total return of the territory.

Still it must be remembered that there were genuine psychological and moral obstacles in the 1970s and 1980s, that prevented Israel from initiating peace talks with the Palestinians. Most important was the Palestinians' and (with the exception of Egypt) the Arab states' refusal to recognize Israel's right to exist, coupled with its two most dramatic corollaries: Palestinian and other Arab terrorism, and the Palestinian intifada, which broke out in December 1987. Other serious obstacles were the ideological, strategic, and tactical divisions among the various militant Palestinian factions and groups, and the absence of overall Palestinian political cohesiveness and unity, which made it difficult or impossible for a particular leader or particular leaders to speak authoritatively for the Palestinian masses in any potential talks with Israel. The removal of these obstacles by the Arab states' recognition of the PLO, with Yasser Arafat at its head, as the sole representative of the Palestinian people, and Yasser Arafat's effective end to PLO terrorism in 1989,[9] helped pave the way for the Madrid Conference, which started in 1991, and the bilateral negotiations between Israel and the Arabs begun in Madrid, and continued, with interruptions, in 1992 and 1993. In 1993, the secret Israel-PLO negotiations in Oslo "culminated in the signing of Israel-PLO Declaration of Principles in Washington, D.C. on September 13, 1993. As part of the arrangement, Israel recognized the PLO as the representative of the Palestinian people. For its part, the PLO recognized Israel's right to exist in peace and security, accepted United Nations Security Council's Resolutions 242 and 338, and renounced the use of terrorism and violence."[10]

I have briefly talked about various potential opportunities for the resolution of the Palestinian Problem that in my view, Israel and the Palestinians had, until very recently, unfortunately missed. By their outright rejection of the UN Partition Plan, the Palestinian leaders and the Arab states themselves missed the century's greatest opportunity to prevent the Palestine Problem from growing into the well-nigh intractable problem it has since become.

The difficulty Arabs and Israelis have of forgetting and forgiving the near-century-long conflicts and hatreds, together with the marked differences in their long histories and experiences, attitudes, mores and values, should not make us despair of the possibility of the peaceful coexistence of Palestinians and Israelis as good neighbors when the former become masters of their own destiny. The present scars and historical differences should not make us forget that, in addition to being morally right and legally just, Palestinian statehood is *the only practical avenue to lasting peace between the two peoples.* But to break out, peace demands "no less than everything" from those who desire peace. Given enough time and effort for the passions on both sides to cool, and the memories of conflict and war gradually to fade with the coming of new generations of Palestinians and Israelis, it is far from impossible for them to live side by side in peace. The peaceful albeit unequal coexistence between Israeli Arabs and Israeli Jews in Israel for the past 50 years should be one cause for optimism. Recent history has also shown that erstwhile adversaries can peacefully coexist—and even, as with the Germans and the French and British—can become part of an increasingly closer economic and financial, cultural, and even political, union.

The peaceful coexistence of Palestinians and Israelis needs to be advanced by common economic and various cultural endeavors and relationships, such as those sketched in chapters 5 and 6, and, it is hoped, facilitated by increasing political liberalization and democratization in the Palestinian state and in the rest of the Arab Middle East.

The peace dividend described in chapter 6 dwelt on the potential long term economic, artistic, and cultural benefits of a comprehensive Arab-Israeli peace, leaving aside the potential benefit that the Palestinians and other Arabs can derive from an appreciation of Israel's political system. I shall briefly focus on this, additional potential dividend of peace.

In chapter 7 I concurred with those scholars who argue that liberal democracy in the Arab countries is likely to further the cause of peace between them and Israel, and argued that democracy would also contribute to their peoples' welfare and well-being. But to become a worthy model, Israel's political-legal system must guarantee, among other things, in practice, the equal human and civil rights of all its citizens, irrespective of ethnic, religious or other differences or allegiances, purging the society of discrimination against the Israeli Arabs and Jews who are now relegated to second-class citizenship.

An independent Palestine existing on *equal terms* with Israel, in the context of a comprehensive Arab-Israeli peace, should help eliminate, in the long run, a main obstacle to Israel's playing the positive political role described; viz. the taint of Israel's occupation of the West Bank and Gaza Strip, southern Lebanon, and the Golan.

Among Arabs, Palestinians have the very best opportunity to create a liberal democratic political and liberal economic system, either at the time of independence or soon thereafter, by drawing up, and implementing, a liberal democratic Constitution and Bill of Rights. Eventual membership in a regional, or expanded European, Common Market which includes Israel *may* also help the new state on the road to democracy. Likewise, *mutatis mutandis*, with the other Arab states.

On the negative side, the checkered history of Palestinian struggle for self-determination, especially since 1967, particularly since the inception of partial autonomy, and the crying need for security within the new Palestinian state and in its relations with Israel, would tend to favor—at least in the foreseeable future—a strong authoritarian government not unlike the present Palestinian Authority. Only if Hamas and Palestinian Islamic Jihad give up the use of force as a means to their political ends, and are transformed into a political opposition party or opposition parties, would the ideal of the sovereignty of the people have an even, or better than an even, chance of realization. The political transformation of the rejectionist elements of Palestinian society should also advance amicable Israeli-Palestinian relations.

The potential for the blossoming of democracy in Arab Middle Eastern countries, in the near future, is appreciably less than in the case of Palestine, given that political authoritarianism is well entrenched in most of them. But continued liberalization and democratization—indeed, liberal democracy—are not out of their reach in the long run, if the conditions for them, some of which were tentatively outlined in chapter 7, are satisfied.

Finally, given an undivided future Jerusalem allowing free, safe movement between the old and new parts of the city to the many ethnic and religious groups that move and have their being there; and given the renovated Jewish Quarter cheek by jowl with the Muslim, Christian, and Armenian Quarters within the Walls, one can foresee a return to the kind of generally relaxed and friendly Arab-Jewish relations in the city as a whole which existed at times during the British Mandate. Then the Old City can perhaps return to its true, historic role as a (or the) spiritual and religious center of the three great monotheistic religions, and become once again a living symbol of amicable and cooperative living for Israelis and Palestinians in particular and Arabs and Jews in general. Nay—a Holy City once again—Jerusalem would radiate peace and good will to the entire world!

As I write, the prospects for a peaceful end to the drawn-out Arab-Israeli conflict appear to be better than practically any time in the last fifty years. Both Ehud Barak and Yasser Arafat are anxious to move the peace process forward, notwithstanding Arafat's present disagreement with Barak's proposal to include the implementation of the Wye Agreement in the final settlement negotiations.[11] Whether the "squabble" will turn into a full-fledged crisis, or even a Netanyahu-style stalemate, is too early to tell, but seems unlikely.

The Israeli leader is also anxious to resolve the dispute with Syria over the Golan Heights, and with Lebanon regarding the Israeli security zone in southern Lebanon, at a time when Syria's Assad appears to be determined to "strike a deal with Israel."[12] Meanwhile, a rival PLO faction, the Popular Front for the Liberation of Palestine (PFLP), which has hitherto opposed the Oslo Accords, has "moved toward reconciliation" with the PLO, as Arafat tries to "build strength for the last stage of negotiations with Israel."[13] It is not unlikely that, as the article states, the PFLP's leaders' new-found realism, in conceding that the Accords have to be "dealt with as a political reality," is a result of their awareness (like other Damascus-based anti-Arafat factions), that if Syria strikes a peace deal with Israel, they may eventually be "expelled from Syria," and so, "will need Arafat's support."[14]

Notes

1. "Israel's biblical roots surface at 50th birthday party," *Milwaukee Journal-Sentinel*, May 1, 1998.

2. Despite its familiar limitations and defects, Palestinian autonomy itself constitutes clear evidence that Israel has indeed "veered toward peace," no matter that autonomy is far from what the Islamists understand "veering toward peace" to involve or mean.

3. "Barak has enormous job ahead of him," *Milwaukee Journal-Sentinel*, July 29, 1999.

4. Oxford, 1991.

5. Ibid., jacket blurb.

6. *Arab-Israeli Conflict and Conciliation, A Documentary History*, Bernard Reich, ed. (Westport, CT, 1995), 146. The Framework, which is strikingly similar to the Oslo Accords, included "transitional arrangements for the West Bank and Gaza for a period not exceeding five years. In order to provide full autonomy to the inhabitants, under these arrangements the Israeli military government and its civilian administration will be withdrawn as soon as a self-governing authority has been freely elected by the inhabitants of these areas to replace the existing military government. . . . As soon as possible, but not later than the third year after the beginning of the transitional period, negotiations will take place to determine the final status of the West Bank and Gaza and its relationship with its neighbors [and to conclude a peace treaty between Israel and Jordan by the end of the transitional period]" (ibid., 148–149). The Framework earlier spoke of the determination of the parties to "reach a just, comprehensive, and durable settlement of the Middle East conflict through the conclusion of peace treaties based on Security Council resolutions 242 and 338 in all their parts" (ibid., 148), which, in the final settlement, would provide for the "elected representatives of the West Bank and Gaza to decide how they shall govern themselves consistent with the provisions of their [i.e., Egypt's, Israel's, and Jordan's, as well as the Palestinian representatives'] agreement" (ibid., 149). Although the Framework stated that the "solution from the negotiations must . . . recognize the legitimate right of the Palestinian peoples and their just requirements," "based on all the provisions and principles of UN Security Council Resolution 242," it significantly failed to mention Palestinian statehood or independence (ibid., 149).

7. Indeed, the Begin plan, in the 1920s, included not only the whole of erstwhile Palestine but also Trans-Jordan: a plan subsequently rejected by the Haganah, during the last days of the British Mandate.

8. Nevertheless, it is possible that the Israeli government continues to favor the return of the West Bank and Gaza Strip (but not East Jerusalem) to Jordan in some form or other, in the final settlement of the Palestine Problem.

9. Perhaps also his May 1989 declaration in Paris that "the articles in the Palestine National Convention rejecting Israel's right to exist were void" (*Remaking the Middle East*, Paul J. White and William S. Logan, eds. [Oxford: New York, 1997], 265. But it was not until 1998 that the full Palestinian Council formally and finally repealed these articles.

10. Reich, op cit., 229.

11. "Barak, Arafat have their first public squabble," *Milwaukee Journal-Sentinel*, August 3, 1999.

12. "Factions within PLO draw closer as negotiations for peace progress," *Milwaukee Journal-Sentinel*, August 2, 1999.

13. Ibid.

14. Ibid.

Index

Abed, Shurki B., 129–130, 145, 152n.
Abdel Nasser, Gamal, 107
Abir, Mordecai, 109, 114n.
Abu Abbas, 41
Abu-Amr, Ziyad, 70
Abu Dis, 66n.
Afghanistan, 146
al-Araian, Sami, 72ff., 89
Algeria, 117–118, 142
al-Tufayli, Sheik Subhi, 71
Amal, 71
American Middle East policy, 10
Antonius, George, 115
Arafat, Yasser, xi–xii, xvn., 8, 12, 32, 38n., 40–42, 60, 62n., 69, 74, 78–80, 86, 90, 156, 161
Arab
  Islamists, xi,
  League, 104
  nationalism, 142
  states, 158
Arab-Israeli
  conflict, xii, 4, 43, 46, 49, 54, 106, 108, 110, 123, 129, 132–133, 135, 151n.
  Common Market, 117
  Peace, 160
Arab/Muslim World, xiv,
Assad, Hafez, 98, 101–102, 111n., 161
Ashrawi, Hanan, 80
Axis Powers, 7

Balfour, A.J, 2

Balfour Declaration, 1–3, 12, 14n., 22, 43
Barak, Aharon, 88
Barak, Ehud, 55, 64n.–65n., 86, 156, 161
Bedouin
  communitarian form of life, 138
  loyalties, 138, 140
  morality of honor and shame, 141
  societal and cultural forces, 140
  traditions, 139
  values, 138, 140
Begin, Menachem, 16, 65n., 99, 103, 157
Berger, Monroe, 151n.
Beetham, David, 136–138, 140–143, 147, 152n.
Ben-Gurion, David, 27
Biblical Land of Israel, 24, 34
Black September, 53
Bolsheviks, 3
Bosnia-Herzegovena, 51
Bourguiba, Habib, 109
British Government, 5
British Mandate over Palestine, 2, 12, 44, 60, 160
Bush, George, 18n.

Camp David Accords, 116, 157
Caplan, Neil, 71
Carter, Jimmy, 103
Cattan, Henry, 65n.
Chomsky, Noam, 45

Christian
  values and norms, 151n., 61
Christopher, Warren, 102
Clinton Administration, 12, 102
Clinton, William, 18n., 86, 103
Cobban, Helena, 112n.
Collective self-determination myth, 33

Dayan, Moshe, 103
Democracy, xiii–xiv, 42, 129–153
  Capitalist, 152n.
  in the Arab world, 146–147
  Liberal, 136–138
  Western-style, 144–145
Democratization in the Arab World, 123, 129–153
De George, Richard, 33
Deir Yassin, 29–35
Druze, 129

East Jerusalem, 9, 29, 33, 40, 46, 49–50, 54, 57–58, 67n., 104, 108, 155, 157
Egypt, xiii, 52, 92, 99–104, 108–110, 115, 117–118, 121–122, 124, 130, 142–146, 157
Egyptian-Israeli peace treaty, 103
  Borough arrangement proposal, 58–59
Egypt's arms race with Israel, 116
Eisenberg, Zittrain, 71
Ethic/morality of honor and shame, 141, 148
Ethiopia, 109
European Commission, 118, 124
European Common Market, 118–121
Expanded European Common Market, 160

Facade democracy, 149n.
Fahd, King of Saudi Arabia, 108
Faisal, son of Hussein ibn Ali, 4
Faisal, King of Saudi Arabia, 107
France, 3–4, 12, 44, 151n.
Friedman, Menachem, 83
Friedman, Thomas, 66n.–67n., 87–89

Garfinkle, Adam M., 15n.–16n., 62n.

Gaza Strip, xi, 9, 12, 30, 33, 40, 44, 47–48, 51–52, 55, 58, 84, 87, 101–103, 118, 131, 133, 135, 142, 155–157
Gaza City, 64n., 77
Golan Heights. 47–48, 98–102, 110, 112n., 121, 133–135, 160–161
Golden Age of Islam, 115
Grossier, Philip L., 14n.
Gulf Cooperation Council, 118
Gulf States, 104–109, 122, 135–136, 146, 150n.
Gulf War, 8, 53, 65n., 105, 131

Habash, George, 41
Haddad, Yvonne Yazbeck, 72, 80
Haj Amin al-Hussaini, 7
Haganah, 29
Hamas (Islamic Resistance Movement), 53, 60, 70, 72, 81, 85, 90n., 106, 131
Harkabi, Yehoshofat, 43, 50
Harris, William, 111
Hashemite
  dynasty, 53
  regime, 104–105
Hebron, 57, 87
Henry McMahon, Sir, 3
Hezbollah, 11, 71, 95–98, 111n., 158
Holy Land, 27
Human rights, 144
  globalization of, 153n.
Hussaini, Hatem I., 38n., 41–42, 50–51, 62n.
Hussein ibn Ali (Sherif of Mecca), 3–4
Hussein, King of Jordan, 104, 106
Hussein, Saddam, 8, 18n., 53, 135

India, 127n.
Indonesia, 146
Intifada, 8, 11, 71, 156
Iran, 79, 138, 142
Iraq, 79, 122, 126n.
  UN economic embargo on, 137
Islam, xiv, 140–142
Islamic
  Jihad, 54, 70, 72, 131

Index

fundamentalism, 140–142, 152n.
Law, xiv, 88
order, 143
regimes, xiv
state 143, 148
Islamist regime, 65n., 85
Islamist rejectionism, 70–89
Islamists, xii, xiv, 40, 88
Israel, xi, xiii, 1–165
   Israeli rejectionism, 82–89
   -PLO Accords, 104
   Arabs, 133
   military buildup, 116
   invasion of Lebanon, 8, 52, 64n.
   Labor party, 99
   Likud party, 99
   security, 54
   -PLO Declaration of Principles, (1993), 158
   negotiations, 105, 158
   -Syrian conflict, 98

Jaffee Report, 53–55
Japan, 122
Jerusalem, xii,
   future of, 57–61, 75
Jewish
   diaspora, 1, 14n., 43
   immigration, 6
   settlements, xii, 10, 86
   state, xii, 5
Jordan, xiii, 44, 51–53, 99, 104, 108, 121–122, 124, 129–130, 142, 146, 149n.
Jordanian
   army, 18n.
   "mixed" political system, 138
   parliament, 149n.
Judaism, 61

Kahan, Maier, 26, 51
Kass, Ilana & Bard O'Neill, 70, 82, 88–89
Khalid ibn Walid, 23
Khalidi, Walid, 48, 57, 63n., 101
King Abdallah, 6–7, 18n.
King Abdallah II, 53
King Hussein of Jordan, 157

Klieman, Aharon, 105
Kuwait, 8, 104, 138

Lackey, Douglas, P., 56, 66n.
Latin America, 138
Lawrence, T.E., 15n.
League of Nations, 2, 5
Lebanon, xiii, 5–6, 11, 64n., 95–98, 108, 110, 129, 131, 140, 142, 146, 149n., 151n., 155
   Lebanese Civil War, 95
   Israeli "security zone" in, 95–97, 157–158
Legrain, Jean-François, 81
Levi-Strauss, 33
Liberalization in the Arab world, 123, 129–153
Libya, 146
Likud Party, 106,
Locke, John, 21

Madrid Conference, 11
Maier, Kahan, 26, 51
Malaysia, 146
Malmberg, Torsten, 21, 24, 36n.
Marquez, Gabriel Garcia, 138–139
McKinley, William, 9
Meier, Golda, 27
Mendelsohn, Everett, 57–59, 61, 67n.
Mezvinsky, Norton, 42
Middle East
   Common Market, 119–122, 124
   peace, xiii
   virtue-ethic of "caring" and "responsibility, 141
Mubarak, Husni, 106
Muslih, Muhammad, 99–100, 112n.
Muslim fundamentalism, 142
Muslims,
   traditional, mainstream, 143
Morrison-Grady Plan, 7
Morocco,
   "mixed" political system, 138
Mossad, 106

"National home" for the Jews, 5, 23
Navakivi, Jukka, 14n.–16n.
Nazi Germany, 7

Nazi Holocaust, 51
Netanyahu, Benjamin, 12, 48, 76, 90n., 155
Netanyahu goverment, 12, 64n.–65n., 71, 77
"New Palestine," 42–44
Nutting, Anthony, 5

Old City of Jerusalem, 29, 59, 66n., 77, 160–161
Ottomans, 3
Ottoman Empire, 5
Ottoman Turkey, 4
Oslo Accords, 9, 13, 40, 44, 46, 55, 60, 69–71, 73, 81, 88–89, 161
Oslo Declaration of Principles, 80
Orthodox Jews, 87–88

Palestine War (1948), 29
Palestinian
  aspirations, xi, 54
  autonomy, xii, 54, 69, 71, 84, 89
  claims, 22
  Diaspora, 80
  Islamist rejectionism, 70–89
  -Israeli conflict, 53
  Interim Self-Government Authority, 18n.
  -Jewish state, xii, 64n.
  National Authority (PNA), 55, 65n.
  National Council (1988), 49, 69, 72, 75, 81, 84, 89
  police, 53
  Problem, xii, 1, 9, 13,22, 40, 43, 46, 49, 157–158
  refugees, 28, 33, 48–4
  rights, 60
  rule, 64n.
  state, xi, 40, 44, 46, 48, 50, 53–54, 58, 61, 69–70, 79, 85
  statehood, xii, 158
  struggle, 160
Partition, 6, 43
Partition Plan, 8–9, 22, 26, 30–31, 50, 157
Perez, Shimon, 88
Peace, xi, 41
  comprehensive, xi, xiii
  lasting, xi
  proposals for, 39–67
Peel Commission, 7, 17n.
PDFLP, 41
PFLP (Popular Front for the Liberation of Palestine), 41, 84, 161
PLF, 41
PLO, xii, 13, 14n., 32, 40, 42, 44, 50, 60, 63n., 70, 76, 95, 104, 109, 114n., 126n., 157–158, 161
Political liberalization and democratization in Arab Middle East, 159–160
Prince Faisal ibn Hussein, 4, 44
Prophet Mohammed, 57

Quest for peace, xi

Rabbi Irving Greenberg, 55–56, 59, 61
Rabin-Perez administration, 18n., 40
Rabinovich, Itamar, 18n., 37n., 44, 63n., 156
Realpolitik, 14n.
Reich, Bernard, 18n., 63n.
Reconciliation, process of, xi
Rothschild, Lord, 2
Roosevelt, Theodore, 9
Rubinstein, Alvin Z., 4, 16n.

Sabra and Shatila massacres, 157
Said, Edward, 2, 29, 37n., 41, 80, 92n.
Shamir, Yitzhak, 26, 99, 157
Sharon, Ariel, 157
Saudi Arabia, xiii
Sayegh, Fayez, 41, 51, 62n.
Sherif Hussein of Mecca, 3, 15n., 44
Shlaim, Avi, 44
Sourani, Raji, 81
South Lebanese Christian militia, 48
State of Israel
  dezionization of, 42
"Sulh," 85
Sykes-Picot agreement, 3–4, 12, 14n., 44
Syria, xiii, 5–6, 44, 50, 64n., 79, 86, 155, 157, 161

Syrian territorial rights, 56

Territorial rights of peoples and nations, 21–38
Terrorism, 121, 158
Tessler, Mark, and Marilyn Gorbschmidt, 133–136, 143, 150n., 152n.
Tovias, Alfred, 118–119
Transjordan, 7, 44, 157
Turkey, 3, 124

United Nations, 7, 12, 22, 25, 42,
  arms inspectors, 79
  Charter, 25, 56
  Coalition against Iraq (1991), 53
  economic aid to future Palestinian state, 47
  Partition Plan, 1, 6, 13, 22, 39, 50
  Partition Resolution, 9
  peacekeeping force, 47, 53
  UNRWA, 41
  Security Council Resolutions 242 and 338, 19n., 30, 35, 73, 158
Ultra-Orthodox Jews, 88

Unitary Arab-Jewish state, 50–52
United States Special Commission Committee (1947), 7
U.S. military aid to Israel, 10

Vester, Bertha Spafford, 28

Washington, xi
West Bank, xi–xii, 9, 12, 30, 33, 40, 48–49, 51–55, 64n.–65n., 67n., 69, 84, 155, 157
World War II, 1
Weizmann, Chaim, 2, 4, 44
Weizman, Ezer, 155
White Paper (1939), 7
Wye River Agreement, 12–13, 55, 65n., 69–70, 84, 156
War with Israel (1973), 40, 52
West Jerusalem, 57, 59

Yassin, Sheik, 81
Yehoshua, A.B., 82

Zaim, Husni, 44, 63n.
Zionism, 2, 5, 27, 43–44, 62n.